The High Alps in Winter: Or, Mountaineering in Search of Health

Elizabeth Alice Frances Hawkins-Whitshed Le Blond, Mrs. Aubrey Le Blond

Nabu Public Domain Reprints:

You are holding a reproduction of an original work published before 1923 that is in the public domain in the United States of America, and possibly other countries. You may freely copy and distribute this work as no entity (individual or corporate) has a copyright on the body of the work. This book may contain prior copyright references, and library stamps (as most of these works were scanned from library copies). These have been scanned and retained as part of the historical artifact.

This book may have occasional imperfections such as missing or blurred pages, poor pictures, errant marks, etc. that were either part of the original artifact, or were introduced by the scanning process. We believe this work is culturally important, and despite the imperfections, have elected to bring it back into print as part of our continuing commitment to the preservation of printed works worldwide. We appreciate your understanding of the imperfections in the preservation process, and hope you enjoy this valuable book.

THE HIGH ALPS IN WINTER;

OR,

MOUNTAINEERING IN SEARCH OF HEALTH.

LONDON:
PRINTED BY GILBERT AND RIVINGTON, LIMITED,
ST. JOHN'S SQUARE.

Mrs. F. Burnaby.

THE
HIGH ALPS IN WINTER;

OR,

MOUNTAINEERING IN SEARCH OF HEALTH.

BY

Mrs. FRED BURNABY,

MEMBRE CLUB ALPIN FRANÇAIS, SECTION DU MONT-BLANC.

London:
SAMPSON LOW, MARSTON, SEARLE, & RIVINGTON,
CROWN BUILDINGS, 188, FLEET STREET.
1883.

[*All rights reserved.*]

PREFACE.

In the summer of 1881 I came to Chamonix for the first time. I arrived there in bad health. As for mountaineering, I knew nothing of it, and cared less. However, after a fortnight spent in the fresh mountain air, I was, one day, induced by some friends to accompany them to Pierrepointue. The weather was fine, the glacier above looked inviting, Miss H—— and I continued to Grands Mulets. The excursion did not tire me, and a week later I returned there to ascend Mont Blanc. Bad weather prevented me reaching the top, and I left Chamonix soon afterwards.

On the 10th of June, 1882, I was once more installed in my old quarters at the Hôtel d'Angleterre. Not with any intention of mountaineering, however. But before long the desire to "go up something" grew too strong to be resisted. Still I did nothing worthy of note. During that season my only ascents were Mont Blanc (on a cloudless day), and the Aiguilles of Belvedere and of Tacul, till a trifle changed all my ideas. A friend had crossed Mont Blanc from the Italian side, by the Aiguilles Grise, and, in answer to my question as to how he had enjoyed the ascent, he answered, "It was such a bore! I would not do it again to save my life!" This reply was certainly not an encouraging one. Nevertheless it had the effect of inducing me to follow his example. Two days later I crossed the Col du Géant to Courmayeur, and then returned to Chamonix by Mont Blanc. In spite of rocks glazed with ice, an endless amount of step-cutting on the slopes, and a second caravan behind who dawdled in a manner sorely trying to my patience,[1] for we could not advance alone without dislodging stones upon their heads, I enjoyed myself immensely. A week later I ascended the Grandes Jorasses. I have placed an account of that excursion in the opening chapter. All the other excursions mentioned took place during the winter of 1882-83. At the end of October I spent another fortnight at Chamonix, but left on November 1st, *viâ* the Col and Aiguille du Tour, for Montreux, disgusted with the continued bad weather. Six weeks of damp on the borders of the lake of Geneva proved too much for me. In spite of kindly warnings against ten feet of snow, starvation, isolation, dulness and many other evils, I returned to Chamonix on the 18th of December,

---

[1] This, however, was owing to the incompetence of the guides. The gentleman whom they accompanied climbed admirably. We dared not keep far in front, the danger of dislodging stones which might fall on those below was too great.

and I did not regret it. Two days later I began my winter ascents.

Should those who may follow in my steps consider that things are in some cases exaggerated, in others made too little of, let them remember that all winters are not alike. That during 1882-83 much snow fell, sometimes facilitating, but oftener rendering more difficult the ascents undertaken. As I found the mountains, so I present them to my readers. It has been my invariable practice to always employ the very best guides, and many obstacles were, no doubt, overcome by the skill of the men who accompanied me. Should mountaineering in winter become popular, as it deserves, numerous inconveniences which I encountered will be avoided. Châlets and mountain inns will be inhabited, roads kept in good order, and diligences will ply between headquarters and the larger towns; guides, too, will be more accustomed to travel in those regions in winter, and to give information regarding the ascents at that season.

I will only add, "Try mountaineering in winter, and you will not be disappointed."

HOTEL DU MONT-BLANC, CHAMONIX,
March, 1883.

For those who, though not themselves mountaineers, yet take an interest in the pursuit, and care to read these pages, I add the following explanation of mountaineering terms used in this book.

Arête.—A ridge, or knife edge.

Bergschrund.—The last crevasse before quitting a glacier and taking to the rocks. Bergschrunds are invariably found at the foot of couloirs.

Col.—A passage between two peaks.

Couloir.—A gully, generally filled with snow or ice.

A Corniche occurs on the crests of many high mountains and cols, and is produced by the action of the wind on the snow, forming it into a wave, which rolls over and overhangs the slope below.

Glissade.—To slide. For a standing glissade the axe or alpenstock is placed behind, in a slanting position, and leant on heavily. For a sitting glissade it is used in almost the same manner. The latter is resorted to when the snow is too soft to allow an upright position to be maintained.

Ice-fall.—A mass of séracs, produced by the unevenness of the rocks over which the glacier passes, causing it to split up into blocks of ice which often take most fantastic shapes.

Moraine.—The *débris* of glaciers, consisting of earth and stones. This *débris* is thrown up on each side of a glacier as it advances, and pushed forward below at its termination.

Serac.—A gigantic block of ice, produced by the unevenness of the rocks below, which splits up the glacier.

Schrund.—A large crevasse.

CONTENTS.

CHAPTER I.

ASCENT OF THE GRANDES JORASSES AND TWENTY-FOUR HOURS IN THE SNOW.

PAGE

A dangerous couloir—Absence of cooking utensils—A magnificent view—Hurried descent—Benighted—The end of our candle—A weary night—The cabin at last—Mr. Whymper's escape from an avalanche 1

CHAPTER II.

FIRST PASSAGE OF THE "COL DU TACUL."

Fog at Geneva—Weather at Chamonix magnificent—Decide for Col du Tacul—My reasons

—Beauty of Montanvert in winter—The couloir at last—A hard bit of climbing—Return to Chamonix—Start for Mont Blanc—Doubts as to weather—Condition of the Grands Mulets—Start for the summit—Involuntary gymnastics—Obliged to turn back—A formidable jump—Descent from Pierrepointue . 19

CHAPTER III.

COL DES GRANDES MONTETS AND ASCENT OF THE AIGUILLE DU MIDI.

Start for Col des Grandes Montets—A weird repast—Curious walls of snow—Original effect of the frost on the Aiguille—Excursions from Lognon—Ascend to Montanvert for Aiguille du Midi—Bad snow—Séracs easy—An endless valley—Slippery rocks—View from the Aiguille—A brilliant sunset—A long day . . . 41

CHAPTER IV.

COL DE CHARDONNET.

A joke produces an important decision—More

gymnastics—Tournier's little dog—A high wind—The Cabane d'Orny—The valley of desolation—Balley—We return from the Cantine de Proz—Tête Noir in winter—Premature sympathy 59

CHAPTER V.

COL D'ARGENTIÈRE.

A winter's day at Lognon—Cupelin's gymnastics—Our tea freezes—Great excitement before arriving on the Col—" Le diable est mort "—Some difficult rocks—A deserted village—Nine miles through deep snow—We astonish the natives—Fresh projects 77

CHAPTER VI.

A JOURNEY IN THE VALLEYS.

Decide for Matterhorn and Monte Rosa—Signor Sella's winter ascent of the former—Ice avalanche on the road to Geneva—At Bonneville—A dexterous porter—Montreux—Incident at Martigny—From Orsières to Liddes—Cupelin manufactures two sledges—Arrival at St. Pierre 93

CHAPTER VII.

THE GRAND ST. BERNARD.

Signs of bad weather—A ferocious dog—The monks in winter costume—I fail to discover the entrance to the hospice—A new dish—An amusing descent—" La glissade de Madame "—The Italian custom-house — Cupelin's fourteen pockets—A runaway mule—No carriages at Aoste—The heat of the valley—Arrival at Chatillon — Disastrous tidings. . . . 113

CHAPTER VIII.

CHATILLON TO VALTOURNANCHE.

Jean-Antoine Carrel—Plans to outwit the Italian caravan—A true mountaineer—The weather continues to get worse—Lack of provisions at Valtournanche—The return of the enemy . 131

CHAPTER IX.

COL ST. THÉODULE.

Signor Sella—We decide to ascend Monte Rosa together—Cupelin finds a chicken—Start for Breuil—The Matterhorn—Aspect of the hut—Difficulty in getting in—The shortest passage of the Matterhorn—Strange dishes—*En route* for Monte Rosa 143

CHAPTER X.

MONTE ROSA.

Descent of a sérac—The Italian guides don't like it—A tiresome plateau—Intense cold—A violent hurricane—Signor Sella's guides refuse to continue—My nose gets frost-bitten—We turn back—We are photographed—We say good-bye to the others—Our reasons for leaving the Matterhorn alone—Arrival at Zermatt—Biner—A—— comes down—Our sledge overturned—We miss the train at Visp—The Salvan *versus* the Tête Noir—Return to Chamonix 157

CHAPTER XI.

CONCLUSION.

The difference between winter and summer in the Alps—Best provisions to take—My method of preventing the wine from freezing—Many drawbacks which will be removed should mountaineering in winter become popular—A tribute to the ability of my guides . . 177

APPENDIX.

A.—Cold *versus* heat as a cure for consumption 185
B.—Mountain walkers and valley walkers . 190
C.—Chamonix in winter 192
D.—The Aiguille du Tacul 194
E.—The rope 196
F.—Condition of the snow in winter . . 198
G.—Hotels and inns in the Alpine valleys . 200
H.—A high level route along the chain of Mont Blanc 201
I.—A few words of caution . . . 203

LIST OF ILLUSTRATIONS.

	PAGE
PORTRAIT OF THE AUTHOR . . .	*Frontispiece*
COL DU TACUL	22
MONT BLANC	32
TRAVELLING ON THE GLACIER . . .	113
TEN MINUTES' HALT FOR BREAKFAST .	161

MAPS.

Chain of Mont Blanc.

Chain of Monte Rosa.

CHAPTER I.

ASCENT OF THE GRANDES JORASSES AND
TWENTY-FOUR HOURS IN THE SNOW.

THE HIGH ALPS IN WINTER;

OR,

MOUNTAINEERING IN SEARCH OF HEALTH.

CHAPTER I.

ASCENT OF THE GRANDES JORASSES AND TWENTY-FOUR HOURS IN THE SNOW.

A dangerous couloir—Absence of cooking utensils—A magnificent view—Hurried descent—Benighted—The end of our candle—A weary night—The cabin at last—Mr. Whymper's escape from an avalanche.

THE Grandes Jorasses is, probably, well known to those of my readers who have visited Montanvert. From the Mer de Glace it looks like a huge pyramid, whose perpendicular walls close the view towards Italy, and frown down in solemn grandeur

B

to the glacier at its feet. Utterly unassailable it appears from that side. And, in truth, it is so; for would the tourist attain its lofty summit, it is from Courmayeur that he must make the ascent.

Towards the middle of September I found myself in that pretty village. The weather was fine, for a wonder, as the summer until then had been so miserably wet. I had just returned from a visit to the hospice of the Grand St. Bernard, and was very anxious to ascend the Grandes Jorasses before the weather changed. It was a source of regret that there was no time for me to telegraph to Chamonix for my guide, Edouard Cupelin. However, I engaged Proment, of Courmayeur, and two porters, and told them to be ready to set out at eight o'clock next morning. As we were starting, another caravan filed out of the town. They were bent, it appeared, on a very different errand to ours. Their object being to breakfast in the pine woods a few miles farther up the valley. Several ladies in gorgeous apparel were of the party, and a porter marched in front, with an enormous hamper of provisions balanced on the top of his knapsack, and a heavy basket in each hand. He gazed enviously at my followers, bound for the cool and snowy upper regions; and they chaffed him on his pleasant occupation. Our way led up through dark woods and past beds of wild strawberries. The fruit looked deliciously cool, and we gathered a quantity for our dinner. The berries were larger than any I had seen before, growing wild; and the luxurious vegetation forcibly reminded one of the difference of temperature on the Italian side of the range. For Courmayeur, though 500 feet higher than Chamonix, is much warmer; and well do I remember, when crossing the Col du Géant, the unpleasant sensation of descending into the valley on the other side! It felt like the atmosphere of a Turkish bath. Once above the woods, a piece of morraine had to be ascended, and then a most objectionable little couloir. It has formed where the border of the glacier hangs over a large inclined slab of rock. Stones fall continually from the overhanging ice. This place cannot be avoided by all the party, but when one guide has mounted he can let down the rope over the face of the cliff,[1] and the rest can scramble up by its aid. A stone fell just before I passed, and another immediately afterwards. On observing this occurrence, I resolved when descending to make the guides lower me down the face of the rock, so as to avoid this spot.

The cabane was reached a few minutes later—a comfortable little place, new and clean. There was also some hay, which was a luxury after the hardness of the boards in the cabane on Les Aiguilles Grise.

[1] A fixed rope would be useful at this spot, and a few notches in the rocks for the feet.

One drawback, however, was quickly discovered. All the cooking utensils had been stolen! We had plenty of tea, coffee, and soup in jelly with us, but how were we to heat it? This was a puzzle. We had not brought a spirit lamp; and a tiny cup and three spoons was all that remained in the cabin. At last a brilliant idea occurred to one of the guides. We had two wine gourds with us. One would be sufficient for the next day. They could cut the side out of the other, and do the cooking in it. The plan succeeded admirably, and supper was soon simmering on the fire. Next morning, at two o'clock the weather was rather uncertain. But at 3.30 the fog, which had been hovering about, cleared off, and we started. A piece of candle—enough for an hour or two, was carried by one of the guides. Note well this fact, for thereby hangs a tale! At first the snow was hard, but it soon turned to ice; and, even before reaching the first rocks, our axes had begun their work. The lower rocks finished, a steep slope had to be crossed—so steep that hand-holes as well as steps were required. The progress was rather slow. I was not accustomed to my guides, and they were not accustomed to me. They often did not know where I required a helping hand and where I could move alone. More rocks were ascended, then another long, steep slope of ice, and it was not till 11 a.m. that we, at length, stood upon the summit.[2] The mist had come on soon after we left the cabin. However, it lifted for a moment, and by advancing to the edge of the corniche, I had a good view. Far below, the graceful windings of the Mer de Glace were seen; and, on its left bank, the hotel of Montanvert showed distinctly. Across the icy sea, the dark lines produced by the unevenness of its progression, were very well marked, and made me think of Mark Twain's

[2] The summit of the Grandes Jorasses is 13,800 feet above the level of the sea.

amusing description of his journey on the Gorner glacier, when he placed himself in the middle to descend by " express " to Zermatt, and the luggage at the side, " par petite vitesse." But to return to the view. To the right, the majestic form of the Aiguille Vert immediately caught the eye; it seemed almost on a level with our standpoint, and overtopped everything else at that end of the range. While, to the left, the great white dome glittered in a stray sunbeam above an ocean of fleecy clouds. The misty curtain was once more drawn down, and we started in hot haste for the descent, as it was most important to reach the cabane before dark. Not once did we stop,[3] and yet, just as we were getting off the last rocks, the night overtook us. Our bit of candle remained, but what a small piece it seemed, with which to do the hour and a half

---

[3] Some time was, however, wasted; for the guides tried a short cut, which entailed a good deal of cutting and several " mauvais pas," which I should not wish to pass again.

which must elapse before we could hope to reach the cabin! We economized it as long as we could. At first we had our steps in the ice to guide us, and could feel for them with our feet. Then came hard snow, crevasses abounded, and we had to light our precious candle. For half an hour we descended by its light, walking as fast as we could; but the numerous "shrunds" took up a great deal of time, and, all too soon, our light began to flicker. Tenderly we placed it on the head of an ice-axe, carefully gathering all the drops of grease around its wick. On we pressed. Would the glacier never end? We were just crossing a large crevasse, my turn had come to crawl over the frail snow bridge when our candle went out, and, once more, darkness overtook us! We wandered about for some time longer (during which I mentally registered a vow that nothing should ever induce me to make another ascent without Cupelin). Then my fears got the better of me. I declined to advance a single step further! The porter behind me muttered, "Better make a night of it here, than break our necks in a crevasse!"

The others said that it certainly would be wiser to remain where we were.

"If madam won't be frozen?"

"Certainly I shall not," I answered.

The night was warm. The fog prevented there being any wind. We began to arrange for our impromptu-bivouac. First a deep hole was dug in the snow. One knapsack was placed in it for me to sit on. I took off my boots, wrapped a silk handkerchief round my feet, and put them in another. Our stock of provisions was next examined. All the wine was finished, but half a flask of brandy, some meat, and some biscuits, still remained. So we were not so *very* badly off. As for wraps, I had a warm red Indian shawl. After half an hour Proment got impatient. He wanted to take one of the porters, try to find the cabin, and return to us with candles.

I begged him to do nothing rash.

He answered,—

"Nous deux, nous sommes solides, il n'y a pas de danger pour nous!"

It was then 10 p.m. They started with the full length of the rope between them. After twenty minutes they returned; it was impossible to advance at that point. They then tried the other side, and presently called to the porter, who was with me, to come and help them. They were descending a steep slope, with a crevasse at the bottom of it. He put in his ice-axe at the top, twisted the rope round it, let them down, and then returned to me.

What a dull time we had up there. First we talked for half an hour or so on the subject of the good dinner we should have on arriving at Courmayeur. Then we tried to make the others hear us, and find out how they were getting on.

"Pas trop bien!" they called in answer.

"It's no good our worrying about them," said my porter. "They will arrive all right in time. If madame would have some supper?"

The idea was a good one; out came the eatables, and ample justice was done to them. Supper concluded, I tried to get a little sleep. The porter, too, arranged himself as comfortably as circumstances would permit, his head on the wine gourd, and the boots which I had taken off, under him. Very strange it seemed, every time I opened my eyes, to see that wilderness of snow around me, and to think, "Here we must remain until some one comes to fetch us."

At last I dozed off. On awakening it appeared to me that I had slept for some hours. I determined to keep awake in case the others should call, for it was important that we should be ready to answer. As I was turning this over in my mind, a cry was heard. I jumped up, dropping the flask off my knee and on to the nose of the porter, who screamed, thinking that it was an avalanche. Below shone a light. It advanced steadily, and, at 3 a.m., our companions arrived, well provided with candles. We went down at once to the cabin, and got there at 4.30.

How comfortable it seemed after our primitive lodging in the snow! I threw myself on a bundle of hay, and slept soundly for two hours. Then we started for Courmayeur. On arriving at the top of the little couloir, I announced my intention of being let down the face of the rock.

"Mais, madame, il n'y a pas de danger!" said the guides.

"Danger or not, I decline to pass that couloir," I answered.

Seeing that I was determined, Proment prepared to lower me over, and seated himself at the top, getting good leverage for his feet against a projecting piece of rock. The rope was then uncoiled. I tied myself to the end of it, and he proceeded to launch me over the edge. The following moment was not a blissful one. I knew that the rope was strong, still my position was not pleasant. It was with relief that I felt my feet once more arrive on the ground. I undid the rope, Proment gathered it up, and ran down the couloir to join me. Two seconds after he passed it a mass of gigantic stones fell from the ice above.

"Ah! quelle chance!" he exclaimed.

"Mais, vous savez, il n'y a pas de danger!" was my reply.

We continued our way towards Courmayeur. The weather was perfectly tropical, and a long halt was made in the pine wood, and several more pounds of strawberries devoured. I found that considerable anxiety had been felt in the town in consequence of our prolonged absence, more especially as no light could be seen in the cabin on the second night.

I can thoroughly recommend the ascent of the Grandes Jorasses to all mountaineers of tolerable ability. The rocks are charming, solid, and giving good foothold and handhold. The ice-slopes are steep, as I have said before, and would be very risky after fresh snow. Those who have read Mr. Whymper's "Ascent of the Matterhorn" will remember the little incident which happened to him during the first ascent of the Grandes Jorasses. "The slopes were steep and covered with new-fallen snow, flour-like, and evil to tread upon. On the ascent we had reviled it, and had made our staircase with much caution, knowing full well that the disturbance of its base would bring down all that was above. In descending, the bolder spirits counselled trusting to luck and a glissade; the cautious ones advocated avoiding the slopes, and crossing to the rocks on their farther side. The advice of the latter prevailed, and we had half-traversed the snow, to gain the ridge, when the crust slipped, and we went along with it. 'Halt!' broke from all four, unanimously. The axe-heads flew round as we started on this involuntary glissade. It was useless, they slid over the underlying ice fruitlessly. 'Halt!' thundered Croz, as he dashed his weapon in again with superhuman energy. No halt could be made, and we slid down slowly, but with accelerating motion, driving up waves of snow in front, with streams of the nasty stuff hissing all round. Luckily, the slope eased off at one place, the leading men cleverly jumped aside out of the moving snow, we others followed, and the young avalanche which we had started, continuing to pour down, fell into a yawning crevasse, and showed us where our grave would have been if we had remained in its company five seconds longer."

CHAPTER II.

FIRST PASSAGE OF THE "COL DU TACUL."

CHAPTER II.

FIRST PASSAGE OF THE "COL DU TACUL."

Fog at Geneva—Weather at Chamonix magnificent—Decide for Col du Tacul—My reasons—Beauty of Montanvert in winter—The couloir at last—A hard bit of climbing—Return to Chamonix—Start for Mont Blanc—Doubts as to weather—Condition of the Grands Mulets—Start for the summit—Involuntary gymnastics—Obliged to turn back—A formidable jump—Descent from Pierrepointue.

ON the 18th of December, 1882, I arrived in Chamonix for the winter. Nothing could exceed the gloomy appearance of Geneva as we quitted it that morning. It had been enveloped in the thickest and dampest of fogs during the week which I spent there, and the cold was intense.

However, at Châtelard, where I changed the

carriage for a sledge, things began to look brighter
A clear moonlight flooded the valley of Chamonix
as we glided up it, and the brightness of the air was
a delightful contrast to the depressing influence of
the place we had left. At 8.30 we arrived in the
village. My guide was waiting to receive us, and
surveying the barometer with evident satisfaction.

"Un temps superbe, madame!"

"Je crois qu'il faut profiter le plus vite possible n'est-ce pas, Cupelin?"

"Madame, c'était mon idée."

"Bien, à demain!"

The next day dawned, bright and cloudless, save for a white mist which filled the valley. It dispersed before the rising sun, and slowly, as though descending from the sky, the glittering points of the Aiguilles, and the mighty summit of Mont Blanc appeared high up above our heads. Sharper and sharper became the outlines, the delicate blue background grew darker and darker, till at length all haze disappeared from the atmosphere, and everything became distinct.

At the hour named, Cupelin arrived. I was undecided what excursion to begin with. For some months my wish had been to cross what was, perhaps, the one remaining untrodden Col in the chain of Mont Blanc. It was true that it led from nothing—nowhere, but it was so strikingly and aggressively a Col, that some one was sure to cross it some day. Therefore, if *I* made the first passage I should perform three praiseworthy actions. First, I should deprive "somebody else" of it; secondly, I should unite the glaciers of Léchaud and Géant by a passage involving a détour of about five hours from the ordinary route; and thirdly, the Aiguille du Tacul would be ascended by quite a new way.

Now as to where this convenient highway is situated (a sort of "high level route" to the Col du Géant). It is placed between the Aiguille du Tacul and Mont Malet, and I had been to the top of it when ascending the former mountain during the summer. The descent towards the Glacier de Léchaud did not look inviting, and, as I have said, no one had either been up or down that side. My vanity was flattered to think that I might accomplish it in winter. Cupelin believed that "il peut se faire." We proposed mounting from the Glacier de Léchaud, and hoped to find a couloir[1] above a small lateral glacier, which, for want of a better name, I have called the "Glacier du Capucin," after the rocks near at hand.

That afternoon we went up to Montanvert. The snow was hard, and in good condition. We arrived at 5 p.m. The moonlight streamed over the Mer de Glace, and lit up those regions of eternal snow to an exceptional degree of loveliness. The sharply defined points of the Charmoz, and the shapely

---

[1] This couloir is not visible unless the Glacier de Léchaud is ascended for some distance beyond the point at which it is necessary to leave it for the passage of the Col. The photograph facing this page was taken during an excursion devoted exclusively to photographic purposes.

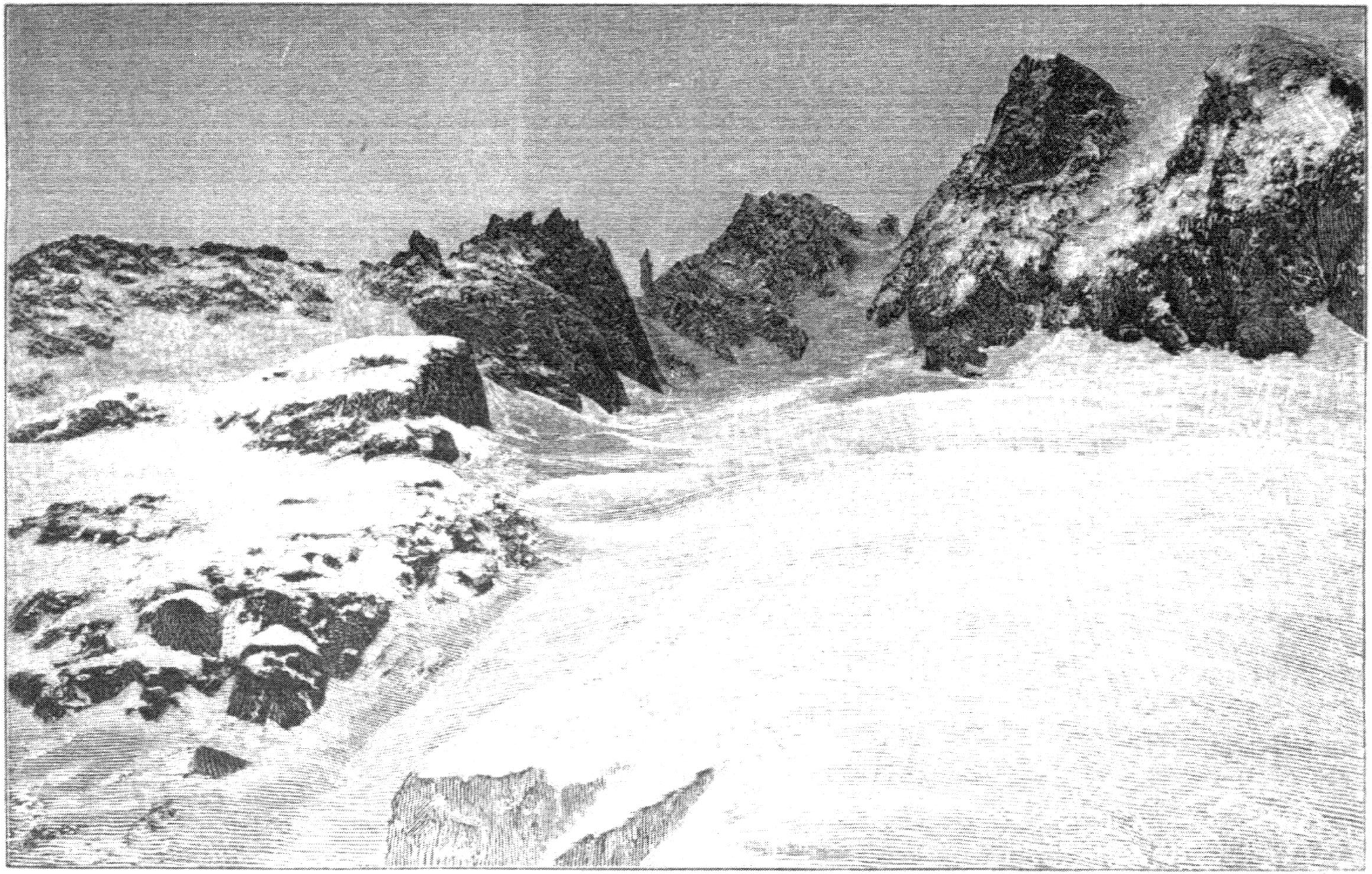

pyramid of the Dru stood out against the sky, while the glistening waves of the glacier nestled at their feet. The start was fixed for five o'clock next morning. A starlit sky greeted us cheerily as we turned out at the appointed hour, and promised a day of no common splendour. A weary cutting along "Les Ponts" followed our departure, and then we kept for an hour on the snow-covered moraine, avoiding the Angle. In front of the Aiguille du Tacul we turned to our left, up the Glacier de Léchaud. At 9.30 we were at the foot of the Glacier du Capucin, and began to ascend on its left moraine. Step-cutting was required till we arrived at the tiny plateau, just above its ice-fall. We placed ourselves near the rocks, and breakfasted. The air was still and warm, the atmosphere wonderfully transparent. Gloves were unnecessary, and warm wraps superfluous. Breakfast over, we proceeded to cross the head of the glacier. Our excitement was intense. Every moment we expected to see our hoped-for couloir, leading up to the Col. If such a couloir existed—good. If not, we were beaten. For the rocks, very smooth at all times, and now, half buried in snow, were out of the question. On we went, our excitement increasing with every step.

"Voilà," I cried, at last, as a glassy-looking wall of black ice came into view.

"Ça commence!" exclaimed Cupelin.

A few yards farther and the centre of our couloir showed itself, steep, icy, guarded by the inevitable bergschrund, but presenting no insurmountable difficulties. A line of blue sky above the snow showed us our destination.

"Tu es mort, tu es mort, Col du Tacul!" cried the guides, and we went to our work with a will; the Col was ours! In a few minutes the bergschrund, half choked with snow, was crossed. Above it our difficulties began. First a few slippery rocks, round which we zigzaged in a manner far from pleasant. Then a steep bit of snow. Our attention was fully occupied, and it was with surprise that, looking up, we saw the Col only about ten feet above us. Ah! those ten feet! They were not to be won so easily. Steeper and steeper grew the slope, a corniche hung over us. We were in the following order. First, Auguste Cupelin, then Edouard, his brother, I was third, and the porter, Michel Saviox, at the end. Auguste crawled under the corniche, and told us to keep our heads down, while he cut it away. We did so, but, getting impatient, I looked up, and received a reminder on my nose, in the shape of a piece of ice, which hurt a good deal at the time, and left a mark for long afterwards. With axes deeply buried in the snow, rope passed round them, and our bodies flattened against the slope, we waited.

At last a loud "hurrah!" announced that Auguste had got his hands over. But it was less easy for him to follow them. However, by aid of violent pushes from his brother's ice-axe, he got up, and was soon dragging us after him. It was done, and our well-known couloir on the other side looked invitingly easy after our late stiff bit of climbing.

I gazed down the slope up which we had come with enormous satisfaction, the more so as we were not going to descend by it! The height of the Col is about 11,000 feet; we only took three hours to ascend from the Glacier de Léchaud. The passage would be very dangerous with bad snow, and an avalanche might easily be started in the steep couloir. The descent was accomplished with ease, and Montanvert reached at 6.30. p.m. Next day we returned to Chamonix, *viâ* the Mer de Glace. The " mauvais pas " was impracticable, and we cut along the slope below, which was a sheet of ice.

I had hoped to start immediately for Mont Blanc, but bad weather set in, and it was not till the 4th of January that there seemed any prospect of my wishes being gratified. On the morning of the 5th we set out, amidst many superstitious forebodings on the part of the domestics of the hotel, for it was a Friday. It was 4.15 a.m. as our little army tramped through the slumbering village. Stars shone above, the air was clear, "but hardly cold enough," remarked the guides. Needless to describe our trudge up to Pierrepointue. Suffice it to say that we found the snow excellent, cut steps for the last hour, and arrived there before eight o'clock. Our spirits had not, however, mounted with the rise in our elevation; for a black-looking layer of clouds which hung over the Jura had given rise to grave uneasiness. A long halt was made at the châlet to ascertain the intentions of the weather.

After an hour and a half things seemed more reassuring. There was little or no wind, excellent snow (so far), and the weather as likely to be fine as not. Can it be wondered, then, that we made up our minds to continue?

On went the rope, and we launched ourselves round the corner, and along the slope of snow which took the place of the path to which the summer tourist is accustomed. A nasty place it would have been with bad snow or less efficient guides. But my men crept along it without flinching, and laughed heartily at my rueful visage. Still, a wall of snow, and a precipice below it which goes down to an invisible depth, are not a pleasant combination, if the timid tourist has to pass along the face of the former like a fly on a window-pane! Five hundred and fifty steps were cut; then we came to the head of the ravine, crossed it, cutting steps this time in solid ice, to the moraine on the other side. Pierre-à-l'échelle was left above, and we took to the glacier at a lower point. All the crevasses were well covered, and the snow still solid. At the Junction the wine went round, we congratulated ourselves on the promising appearance of the weather, and our spirits rose higher and higher as we thought that before twenty-four hours had passed we should be standing on that white mound "(so like a pudding," I once heard a tourist profanely remark), which looked so incredibly near.

A slight damper occurred on mounting the "côte" of the Grands Mulets. There was no doubt of the fact; the snow in the upper regions was simply atrocious!

"Never mind," said Cupelin, "bad snow won't turn *us* back."

Deeper and deeper we sank, till suddenly our comrade at the end of the rope was up to his shoulders.

"What is the matter?" I asked.

"Don't know, madame, but I think it's a crevasse!"

We pulled, and he scrambled on to hands and knees; a chasm yawned below, whose greenish walls of ice went down, it seemed, for ever. A crevasse, true enough, but our only one. We floundered upwards, and presently gained the rocks and the cabin. A quarter of an hour was spent in removing the snow which had drifted against the door. When, at last, we could open it and go in, what desolation met our eyes! Piles of snow on the shelves, a coating of ice on the floor, and everything frozen. Wine bottles smashed from the congelation, the chimney full of snow, and suffocation when we tried to light the fire. Simon poured gallons of petroleum on it, but to no purpose. However, after an hour's work the place began to look more comfortable, and, better than all, the weather was now everything we could wish. Before dark the guides departed to make the tracks *pour sortir des rochers*.

We had arrived at the cabin before 3 p.m. The next morning, at 3.30, the guides knocked at my door, saying, "The weather is lovely;" and adding, "Nous allons tuer la grande machine." The thermometer in my room was at freezing-point during the night. Outside the cabin it stood at thirteen degrees of frost. At half-past four we started. A slight mist had begun to show itself over Geneva, and spread slowly on all sides.

"What do you think of it?" I asked the guides.

"Madame, we hope that the fog may not be serious, but we can't be sure yet."

So we continued to pursue our upward way. On the slope below the Petit Plateau a knapsack was opened to get out our wine. I was third on the rope: something white skimmed past me, and was lost to view.

"Where is the bread?" asked Auguste. "Can we have forgotten it?"

The mystery was explained by what I had just seen. Pursuit was hopeless. We bemoaned its loss, but our stock of biscuits remained.

"And we're not likely to eat much to-day!" remarked Cupelin.

A few crevasses opened under our feet, but the

Grand Plateau was reached at eight o'clock without serious difficulty, though the softness of the snow made the ascent a tiring one. On the Grand Plateau the thermometer marked twenty-three degrees of frost, and a fine snow had begun to fall. Still, however, the mists were light, and we hoped to struggle without risk to our destination. But by what route? Auguste fancied that the Bosses would be best. I also thought so; but the chances of being frozen there were too many, and the idea was abandoned. "The *ancien passage*" would save us two hours, and with good snow we should have undoubtedly chosen it. In the present circumstances this was out of the question. There remained, then, the long and tedious Corridor. We toiled across the Grand Plateau. Endless it seemed on that winter's morning, as our eyes, riveted on the white cone above, enveloped in the lightest of mists, we calculated the chances for and against our fortunes. The slope of the Cor-

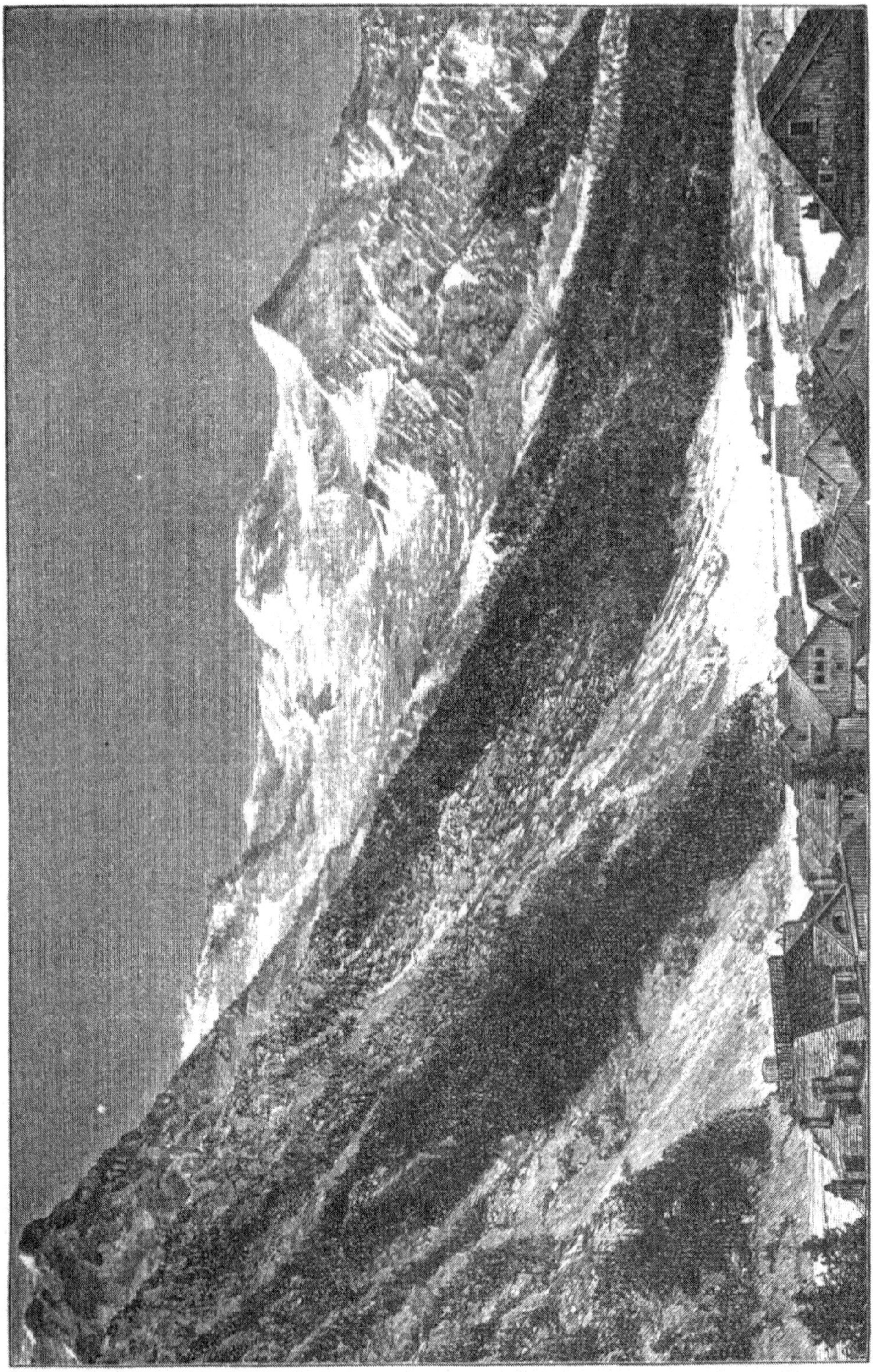

ridor came at last, and we began to mount it; but a mighty bergschrund swept across its entire width, and a single bridge crossed the yawning gulf, and showed us our passage. It was not by any means a solid-looking bridge. Would it bear the weight of a human body? This was the point to be decided. Our leader, Auguste, dropped on his hands and knees to try it. The others kept back, and watched. He safely reached the middle—he was over. But no. For crack!—he and the bridge disappeared. A gap in the snow told us that our leader was below in the crevasse. We pulled; he yelled. We redoubled our efforts, till an exclamation of "Don't pull like that, unless you want to manufacture a tunnel through the bank!" caused us to stop. Cupelin advanced, lay down, and looked over. His brother had fallen on a convenient little ledge, from which, by our mistaken zeal, he had been lifted. The rope had become deeply embedded in the bank, and had, in consequence, pulled him against the side of the crevasse. A little judicious cutting-away of its edge released him, and he got out, none the worse for what the others sarcastically called his gymnastics. For many weeks afterwards they joked him unmercifully on the subject, and it was not till a month later that an opportunity of turning the tables on his brother occurred.

Our bridge gone, another passage had to be found. We glanced up and down, and presently noticed a place where the width was not too great to jump. There was one disadvantage, however. We should have to start from an icy knife-edge above a slope, leading to numerous crevasses, varying from the size of the moat of an ancient castle to that of the interior of the Albert Hall. An upward jump, too, is never agreeable. Never mind; jumped it had to be; and an energetic hop took up our leader, who pulled us after him. The plateau of the Corridor was gained, and two more crevasses crossed, both of which were deep, narrow, and with smoothly-polished sides. As I passed the second of them the sad tragedy which happened at that very spot, resulting in the deaths of poor Mrs. Marks and a porter, occurred to my memory, and I could well realize the awful danger of falling into those gloomy depths when unprotected by the security of a rope.[1] At the foot of the Mur de la Côte cutting began, and continued for an hour. At 1 p.m. we arrived on the plateau. The cir-

[1] Mr. and Mrs. Marks and a sister of the latter, accompanied by two guides and a porter, had started from Grands Mulets to ascend Mont Blanc. On arriving at the Corridor the ladies were tired, and wished to remain there. Mr. Marks continued the ascent with the two guides. Finding the cold trying, the ladies descended a little, and the porter gave his arm to Mrs. Marks, who was greatly fatigued. After a few steps a covered crevasse opened beneath their feet, and they were instantly precipitated to its depths. Mrs. Marks' sister, who was behind, was saved through the breaking of the rope. Her cries caused Mr. Marks at once to return, but nothing could be done for the unfortunate victims, whose bodies were never recovered.

cumstances were not pleasant. A driving snow, a thick fog, thermometer four below zero, and still sinking. A counsel was held. The chances of losing our way during the descent were too many to make it prudent for us to continue, although, from this spot, barely an hour suffices to reach the summit of Mont Blanc. A porter looking back observed that our tracks on the upper part of the Mur were already obliterated. That settled the question. Sorrowfully we turned, and began our downward way. Well was it that we took this resolve. Our steps in the ice remained, it is true, but we had to feel for them with our feet, they were filled with fresh snow. Below, on the Corridor, not a track, not a trace of our passage an hour and half before. Half a foot of fresh snow lay over everything. We pressed on. The bergschrund was reached in the middle, this time, and a little plateau on the other side was waiting to receive us from the slope above. The two porters jumped, one after the other. Then my turn came. I looked across. The distance seemed to have doubled itself.

"Cupelin, I can't jump that!" I exclaimed.

"Over with you, madame!"

I summoned up all my courage. I floundered off my feet, and, after what seemed an age, found myself on the other side. We waded perseveringly down the remainder of our journey, and got to Grands Mulets at 5.30 p.m. But one more little incident took place about an hour before we arrived at our destination. A small crevasse, with a treacherous bridge over it, was in our path. One by one we sat down to cross it, the guide in front pulling the rope of his neighbour who was behind. The rope between me and Simon was loose when my turn came; this he did not perceive in the darkness.

"Tirez!" I cried. He thought that I said, "Ne tirez pas," and did not move.

Crackle! crackle! went the bridge under my weight, as, with my shoulders one side of the crevasse and my feet the other, I tried to balance myself.

"*Tirez!*" I exclaimed, and at last he did so, just as the last remnant of my bridge vanished. Many were his apologies when he saw what had happened, but we thought it time to light the lanterns.

Next morning we left the cabin at eight o'clock. The descent from Pierrepointue to Chamonix was really delightful; one could glissade almost the whole way. The weather had completely changed. It was now bright and clear, but very cold.

CHAPTER III.

COL DES GRANDS MONTETS, AND ASCENT OF THE AIGUILLE DU MIDI.

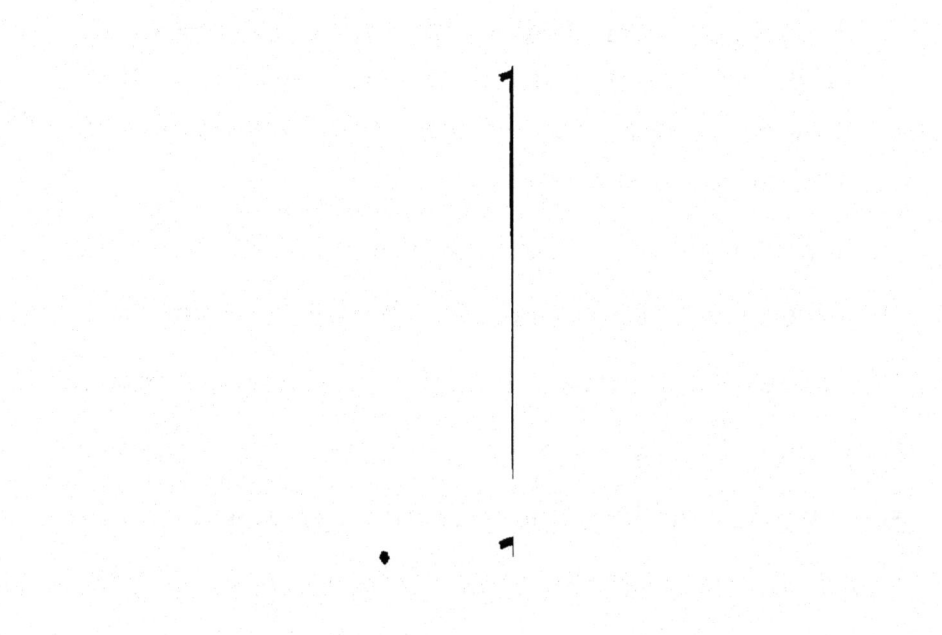

CHAPTER III.

COL DES GRANDS MONTETS, AND ASCENT OF THE AIGUILLE DU MIDI.

"Ce n'est que le premier pas qui coûte."

Start for Col des Grands Montets—A weird repast—Curious walls of snow—Original effect of the frost on the Aiguille—Excursions from Lognon—Ascend to Montanvert for Aiguille du Midi—Bad snow—Séracs easy—An endless valley—Slippery rocks—View from the Aiguille—A brilliant sunset—A long day.

ALL the subsequent ascents which I shall describe in these pages, were made for the first time in winter, unless the contrary is stated. For that reason they were doubly interesting to me. I was never sure, when starting, whether the thing was practicable or not, and this uncertainty gave the excursion a flavour of excitement which was very enjoyable. Besides (shall I be honest enough to admit it?), to do something which no one else has done is pleasant, for the gratification of our vanity has a large share in the proportion of happiness allotted humanity.

But, enough of this moralizing, and let me tell how I crossed the Col des Grands Montets on the 15th of January, 1883. On the morning of that day, at half-past one o'clock, our sledge was rapidly quitting Chamonix for Les Tines. The weather was fine, the sky studded with numberless stars. Many joltings and bumpings were encountered, for but little snow remained on the road. However, 2.30 saw us without any serious mishap a hundred yards or so above Tines. There we got out and started upwards through the pine woods, amidst many fervent "bons voyages" and "good success" from our faithful cocher, Alfred Comte, who, however, often remarked as he drove us to our various starting-points:—

"Ah! the mountains, they're all very well in summer; but at this time of year, I'd rather be in my sledge."

"Would you be afraid, then?" I asked.

"Certainly I should, madam," he answered.

An hour passed, and we found ourselves just below the Chapeau. There the rope went on, our axes fell to work, and it was not till five o'clock that we arrived on the moraine in front of the Hôtel de Montanvert, having cut along below the "mauvais pas" and the slope beyond. The lantern was hung to an ice-axe, we gathered round it, and a hasty breakfast was despatched. The light of the lantern caused the queer blocks of rock to cast weird shadows around us, while the most complete silence reigned in those snowy regions. Not even the fall of an avalanche was to be heard, though many traces of them could be seen. The moraine was furrowed by gigantic stones, which had fallen from the heights during the recent storms, and the

Mer de Glace was strewn with them. No one felt cold; not a breath of wind was stirring. Breakfast over, the real ascent began. A smooth slope of snow stretched from the Col right down to the Mer de Glace, broken only by one obstruction which I shall presently describe. Up this slope we proceeded. The quality of the snow was execrable, but solid enough so far as danger from avalanches was concerned. Now a chamois strayed to very near us, but fled rapidly and with a marvellous agility up the rocks, so soon as he became aware of our presence. The lantern was put out at 7 a.m.; we were then on a level with the Glacier de Nant-Blanc.

"Which couloir shall we ascend?" I asked.

"The one to the right," answered the guides; "it will be better at this season than that generally chosen in summer."

It did not take long to mount, and soon we were on the arête between the two couloirs, in full view of Chamonix, and busily consuming a second breakfast. A gully to the right, steep but short, was our next object; but first as to the obstruction which I have mentioned a page or so back. This curious and unusual phenomenon of nature which we had to avoid consisted of a wall about fifteen feet high, produced, no doubt, by the large accumulation of winter snow. When at Chamonix we had decided that an avalanche had fallen from it. A nearer examination, however, showed that this was not the case; the snow below was smooth and undisturbed. We kept to the left of the gully, and crossed it just above the wall. This brought us to an arête, which I had fondly imagined was the summit. Another rose behind, and then another, till, as I began to think that the point of the Vert was the only true one, the Col and Aiguille des Grands Montets came in sight. At the same moment Chamonix disappeared. From the Col we climbed the Aiguille. I led the way, to the great amusement of the guides, who cheered encouragingly as I sent them down blocks of hard snow from my ice-axe; for here the quality of the snow was completely changed. The wind had done its work, and icicles, which, instead of hanging from the rocks, stood out straight, produced an effect quite new to us all. It was 11.40 a.m. when we reached our goal, and we remained there half an hour. The sky was blue and clear, the distant mountains wonderfully distinct. A fog hung, as usual, over Geneva. Indeed, I have on no occasion during the winter seen that favoured city free from mist. The view was a lovely one, and the white mantle of snow in the valleys made it far more so than in summer. To the North and West it was not, perhaps, a grand scene upon which the eye rested; but the rippling hills towards Salanches, and the rounded summits of the Valais looked very beautiful on that bright January morning. To the East and South a magnificent panorama was spread out, and has been described in glowing terms by Mr. Adams Reilly, to whose account (*Alpine Journal*, No. 6) I refer the reader. Half-past twelve saw us back on the Col, and at two o'clock we were at Lognon. This is an excursion which I can thoroughly recommend in winter to the tourist, who, while not seeking difficulties, wishes to arrive at an altitude of about 11,000 feet. Should his ambition, however, lead him to try something a little less easy, a night may be comfortably spent at the excellent châlet of Lognon after the passage, and the next day he may cross the Col de Chardonnet, Fenêtre de Salena, and return to Chamonix *viâ* the Col du Tour.

When reposing on the Col du Tacul, the Aiguille du Midi had attracted my attention, and it had seemed to me that the ascent of it ought to be quite practicable at this season. A day of unusual magnificence produced in me the restless wish to "do something" on the morrow, and drew me in the direction of Pélérins, where my guide lives. His wife was in, and begged me to wait, as she expected her husband every moment. He turned up presently, and I unfolded to him my plans. My desires soared to the summit of the Aiguille Vert, but much fresh snow had fallen, and prudence counselled a more modest ascent.

"We could do the Aiguille du Midi," suggested Cupelin.

"But it would be such a bore to spend the night on the Col du Géant," I remarked.

"We will do it all from Montanvert," he answered."

"You think that we could?"

"Ma foi, *oui*; et nous le ferons."

The thing was decided; and at 8 a.m. next morning (January 19th), we were trudging up to Montanvert. We started at that hour to allow sufficient time for the guides to make the tracks to the Angle the same afternoon. I rebelled against passing "les Ponts," and they accordingly followed the ordinary Mer de Glace route, and kept along the Moraine. At Montanvert, it was warmer than in the valley, and sitting out in the sun was pleasant. The evening came, and with it the preparations for the following day. My hopes were high, the weather was perfection, and there seemed every prospect of the ascent being a success; the snow was the only drawback.

"Et de ça," said the guides, "nous en aurons assez."

At last silence reigned in the hotel, and every one was engaged in getting the largest amount of rest and renewed vigour in the smallest amount of time. But at midnight the household was once more on its feet. Knapsacks were packed, the rope put on ("ça sera pour longtemps!" remarked the guides), and at ten minutes past one we filed out of the hotel and down the old familiar moraine to the Mer de Glace. There is no need to describe our journey up it. We kept close to its right bank. At the foot of the Tacul the moon waned, our lantern was lit, and we plunged onwards, snow to our knees, and nasty bits of ice, the débris of avalanches from the little glaciers above, beneath our feet. We did not arrive at the foot of the séracs till 5.30. Very easy they seemed. Very different from their condition in summer did we find them. We were untroubled by crevasses. Only three small ones were opened by our leader. Still it was weary work, walking in the dark through deep snow. Seven o'clock brought us a little daylight. We were above the séracs. The lantern was left there, and on we went. On, always on, the snow ever increasing in softness. At last we rounded the Rognon and our Aiguille came into sight.

"Que le bon Dieu nous aide, nous aide. De monter en hiver comme en été!" sang out the guides.

Would the snow be better up there?

We feared not, but hoped to do it " quand même!" as Cupelin remarked tranquilly.

The endless " Vallée Blanche " had to be crossed, and a hot sun on our backs did not make the passage a pleasant one. Below the bergschrund breakfast was partaken of, and the knapsacks and wine-gourds left there. It was one o'clock when we arrived on the arête, and had our first view of Chamonix. The eye plunged straight down to the valley beneath, and the tiny cluster of houses from which so many telescopes were pointed towards the ridge on which we stood. At the end of the arête a pleasant surprise awaited us. For the snow on the Aiguille itself was solid and of an excellent quality. Still I can hardly call the ascension in winter an easy one, even with this advantage. In some places the snow did not lie thick enough to admit of a good step being cut in it. It had in that case to be removed until a ledge was found beneath, and the rocks were then wet and slippery. They were smooth and polished in the Cheminée, and without foothold or handhold for a person of my small stature. I mounted them on my knees, my hands spread out against the rougher portions of the rock. A considerable amount of tugging from above was necessary, and Cupelin, from his lofty perch, looked like a fisherman landing an unwieldy salmon. At last Auguste, who led, exclaimed, "Me voilà!" and in a few minutes we all stood on the top.[1]

Chamonix lay at our feet, and a puff of smoke, followed some seconds later by a "boom," announced that the good people below had seen our arrival, and were firing the cannon in our honour.

It was just two o'clock. Clearer, far clearer, than in summer, was the atmosphere. Everything upon which we gazed was clothed in white, save

[1] The summit of the Aiguille du Midi is 12,600 feet above the level of the sea.

the valley of Salanches, where green fields could be seen. The Graian Alps first caught the eye, as they stood out sharply against the delicate blue background. The pointed Grivola showed well above the range, while, to the left, the unrivalled Matterhorn just lifted his lofty head over the other mountains. The Grandes Jorasses rose straight from the Italian valley below, and reminded me forcibly of the weary hours I had spent on their slopes some four months before. As for Geneva, the fog in that direction would have told us where the town was situated, had we not known where to look for it. For twenty minutes I enjoyed the magnificent view. Then my thoughts turned to more commonplace subjects and my gaze wandered towards the plateau below, and some black objects on it, which meant "knapsacks" and "dinner." We waved an "au revoir" to Chamonix, and the descent began. Soon we were once more on the arête and running gaily down it. No turning out of the toes was needed here; one could have driven a coach and four up it. The arête concluded, a farewell was telegraphed to the crowd below, and we flew towards our luncheon. Having eaten with a good appetite, the route was continued. As we emerged from the Vallée Blanche, the sun set. It was a splendid sight. It did not foretell fine weather, and for that reason the colours were all the more vivid. The Aiguille Vert was capped with crimson, and the fiery hue was reflected on a cloud behind us, to which a dark and and sharply-pointed splinter of rock made a striking foreground. Deeper and deeper grew the shade, till at last but a spark remained, and then all turned to a cold violet. The moon shed presently a welcome light, and, by the aid of her beams we descended the séracs. All our tracks had been obliterated by the wind, and on arriving below Montanvert, our steps were also filled. New ones had to be cut, and it was not till 10 p.m. that the rope was taken off at the hospitable doors of that most excellent hotel. We spent the night there, and while descending to Chamonix next morning wondered what more we could do to make the good people below open their eyes.

CHAPTER IV.

COL DE CHARDONNET.

CHAPTER IV.

COL DE CHARDONNET.

" Something between a hindrance and a help."
WORDSWORTH.

A joke produces an important decision—More gymnastics—Tournier's little dog—A high wind—The Cabane d'Orny—The valley of desolation—Balley—We return from the Cantine de Proz—Tête Noir in winter—Premature sympathy.

WHAT should I do next? It really was not such an easy matter to decide. The question was more, "What could be done?" I did not want to cross the Col du Géant and return by the Talèfre. I had had enough of the Mer de Glace, and was anxious for a change.

"Cupelin, what do you advise?" I asked.

"Madame, we could cross the Col de Chardonnet and Fenêtre de Salena, returning by the Col du Tour."

"The first part of your programme will do," I answered; "but I object to return by the Col du Tour. I don't want to waste my time in doing things which I've done before. Is there no other way of getting back?"

"Madame, we could descend to Orsières and return by the Tête Noir."

"The Tête Noir, Cupelin? If you attempt to make me return by the Tête Noir, I'll make you return by the Col d'Argentière!"

This I said merely in joke; the idea that the latter Col was practicable in winter had not occurred to me.

"Ma foi!" answered my guide, "I'm not sure that it's possible."

"Of course not," I said. "I did not mean it seriously."

"Cependant—cependant," continued Cupelin. "With good snow I don't see why we should not do it."

"Really? Do you really think so?"

"Mais—je le crois."

A little more conversation and my plans were decided as follows. Next day we were to ascend to Lognon. The day after cross the Chardonnet to Orsières. From Orsières the following afternoon to the châlets of La Folie, and, on the third day, regain Chamonix by the Col d'Argentière.

My projects somehow came to the ears of the principal guides of Chamonix. Dear me! What an outcry they made!

"The Chardonnet in winter! It's impossible. As for the Col d'Argentière!—mais ce sont des fous!"

I heard it all with the calmest indifference, and the guides remarked,—

"Nous allons les faire voir quelque chose."

The snow to Lognon was as bad as snow could be. For the Chardonnet it would not matter, but how about the Col d'Argentière? I could only hope that the two intervening days might harden it.

Next morning, February 2nd, we left Lognon at a quarter past four o'clock. We did not light the lantern, as the way was easy. In descending from the Col des Grands Montets we had mounted a slope near the châlet, overhung by a corniche. This we were now approaching.

"We must be somewhere near the corniche by this time, I think," said Cupelin.

As he uttered the words he disappeared. It was too dark for me to see what was the matter, but Cupelin's voice from below, and the laughter of his brother, soon explained what had happened. The latter was now fully rewarded for the teasing he received below the Corridor, and, to this day, Edouard Cupelin has not heard the end of his jump over the corniche of Lognon. Jean Tournier, the courteous proprietor of the châlet, accompanied us to assist in making the tracks. His little dog was also of the party, and ran merrily after balls of snow, or rolled round and round, trying to warm his poor little paws. I think that he enjoyed the excursion far more than his master On arriving at the first plateau of the Glacier d'Argentière the snow suddenly changed, and became of an excellent quality. No difficulties were met with, and, at a quarter past ten, just six hours after quitting Lognon, we stood on the summit of the Col.[1] Stood, did I say? I ought to have written, we crossed it; for a violent hurricane greeted us somewhat roughly on the top, and waves of snow were dashed against our faces. The cold substance pricked like a hundred needles, and even the little dog squealed from pain. We

[1] The summit of the Col de Chardonnet is 11,067 feet above the level of the sea.

at once began the descent of the rather steep slope on the other side. A few minutes later we arrived on the edge of the bergschrund, jumped it, and crossed the plateau of the Glacier de Salena, till we got into the sun and out of the wind. There half an hour's halt was made for breakfast, and at 12.30 we looked through the Fenêtre de Salena.

This little col received its name from its curious shape. It is a passage, only about six feet wide, and connects the glaciers of Salena and Tour. When we started the guides had feared that we should be too late to descend to Orsières the same evening, and that a night at the Cabane d'Orny was inevitable. This I was most anxious to avoid. I had spent the night of the 1st of November there, and had felt the cold acutely. The guides, too, had found it so chilly that they passed the night round the stove, consuming innumerable cups of tea—about twenty-five each, I think! We had burnt almost all the wood, and the rugs, which are kept there in the summer, had been removed just five days before. There was, even then, about three feet of snow round the cabin. However, we were now certain of getting to Orsières that day, so we felt no uneasiness as to our night's lodging. We crossed the monotonous plateau of the Glacier de Trient, and began the descent of the Glacier d'Orny. In a short time we passed one of the pillars of the ruined chapel, but where was the cabin? I looked up and down the bank carefully for some minutes, but not a vestige of it was to be seen. Not even the chimney appeared through the thick layer of snow which was over it. Well was it that we did not depend for shelter on the Cabane d'Orny! We kept along the slope to the left (the ordinary route is to the right), and once beyond the head of the gorge, a glissade brought us down into it. I should much like to describe that gorge as we saw it on the 2nd of February, but, as the guides with truth remarked, no description could convey the idea of what it was to any one who had not themselves seen it. At its head an enormous cascade of green icicles depended from the rocks above. The latter were destitute of snow, for all the avalanche débris which the upper gorge contained had overbalanced itself, and scraped the rocks clean during its downward fall. Below, huge blocks of ice, as large as a house, piled one on the other in the wildest confusion, filled the middle of the valley. On each side of this gigantic dyke (for it had quite that appearance) smaller avalanches had descended the slopes, and strewn the ground with blocks of ice of from two to four feet square. That would have been unpleasant enough to walk on, but, to make things still worse, five inches of flour-like snow covered everything.

For this reason, and in the growing darkness, it was impossible to know when one's foot was secure, and when one could expect to slip. Every moment we sank between the slippery blocks, and loss of temper, and bruises without number, were the result. The progress was of necessity slow, as a sprained ankle would have been inevitable without the greatest caution. Three miserable hours were spent in that treacherous gorge, and it was pitch-dark before we were once more on terra firma. The rope was kept on till we got to the village of Orny. We stopped near a house just outside it to detach ourselves. While we were performing this operation a woman rushed out, exclaiming,—

"Qu'est-ce que vous faites là?"

"We are brigands," answered Cupelin.

"I'm sure you're not, otherwise I should not be here," she replied.

"Ah!" remarked my guide, "then I suppose I'd better tell you the truth. We left Chamonix this morning, and have crossed over the top of the Aiguille Vert and the Col de Chardonnet."

"Ah! a nice excursion," was all the astonishment which she displayed.

"If I'd told her we'd come over the Himalayas, she'd have said the same," growled Cupelin. "Some people know nothing"—a most unanswerable affirmation.

Orsières was reached at 8.20 p.m. The night was fine, but the stars shone almost too brightly. My heart sank at the prospect of bad weather, for, with such good snow in the heights, I had looked upon the Col d'Argentière almost as a certainty. Tournier, however, did not seem depressed; in fact, I think he rather wished to escape the ordeal.

Next day, clouds, mists, and all other signs of a change in the weather. We were simply in despair. Our good snow spoilt. Our return a failure.

"I would give twenty pounds to cross that col," groaned Cupelin.

Till mid-day we lingered on at Orsières, unwilling to leave the object of our affection. The clouds had by that time dispersed to a certain extent. Still, a high south wind in the upper regions told us that fine weather could not be reckoned on, and prudence forbade our spending a night at the châlets of La Folie, when the chances of a storm the following day were so many. Something had to be settled, however. A man, just arrived from the Grand St. Bernard, told us that there was forty-five feet of snow round the hospice. An idea occurred to me.

"Suppose we go to the Grand St. Bernard at once, and return to-morrow? If the weather should be fine we can then continue to La Folie; if not we will return to Chamonix by the Tête Noir."

The guides thought the plan a good one, and we started. Tournier did not accompany us. He confessed that he had had enough of it, and took the post that afternoon to Martigny. We walked quickly up to St. Pierre, and arrived there just three hours after quitting Orsières. A hot sun half roasted us at first, and a piercing wind nearly froze us for the last hour. The well-known guide, Daniel Balley, was in front of the Hôtel Déjeuner de Napoléon, as we got there. We had intended, in any case, to engage him to return with us by the Col d'Argentière, and, now that Tournier had left, it was doubly important to secure him.

" Would he come ? "

" Yes, willingly ; but how about the rocks this time of year ? "

" I engage to get up them, but we must first get to them," remarked Cupelin.

" Oh ! as for that, I'll undertake it," answered Balley.

A capital guide he is ; strong, courageous, and of wide and varied experience.

It was beginning to get dusk as we left St.

Pierre. Balley came with us. The snow was soft and powdery, a high wind drove it into our faces. At last, after two hours, we arrived at the Cantine de Proz. The weather seemed to have quite altered. A clear, starlight night promised well for the morrow.

"Ce n'était qu'un coup de vent," said the guide.

A consultation was held at the Cantine. Balley thought that, if the weather next day were fine, we should not have time to get from the hospice to Orsières, order the provisions, porters with rugs, &c., and arrive at La Folie early enough to make tracks for the following day. To continue to St. Bernard under these circumstances, seemed rather a "penny wise and pound foolish" proceeding. We might, in consequence, miss the Col d'Argentière. We decided to return to St. Pierre. We did so. But alas! during the night it snowed, and all hope for our beloved Col was over. Poor Balley was greatly provoked, it was just the kind of excursion to suit him. Snow fell heavily as we crossed the Forclaz, from the summit of which a long slide took us to Trient. Down there, a fog hung over us, and the air was hot and heavy. Very strange and ghost-like looked the Tête Noir, in its winter garb. Big icicles were hanging from the rocks, and a waterfall below was frozen into a block of green ice. We spent that night at Chatelard, and left early next morning for Chamonix. The mist had cleared off and a cloudless sky took its place. Very downcast did we feel as we approached Argentière. We had done something, but the chief object of our excursion had failed. Above the village a well-known guide met us.

"So you have done the Chardonnet," he said. "I would have bet anything that it was not possible. Of course you could not do the Col d'Argentière; of that we were all quite certain."

When he had passed, I exclaimed, "Cupelin, this is something intolerable, we must do that Col.

Will you come up to Lognon to-morrow, and try it from this side?"

"If madame is not too tired."

"Tired! I could start at once," I answered.

From Lognon the passage is more difficult, the steep part has to be descended instead of ascended. Presently some one else made the pleasing remark, that he "had told us so."

"You imbecile," cried Cupelin. "Can't you understand that the weather stopped us? Our excursion is merely postponed."

"Ah!" said my guide, "every one pities us, and tells us that we shall either break our necks or return by the route we went by. We'll just open their eyes for them the day after to-morrow!"

CHAPTER V.

COL D'ARGENTIÈRE.

CHAPTER V.

COL D'ARGENTIÈRE.

"Where there's a will there's a way."

A winter's day at Lognon—Cupelin's gymnastics—Our tea freezes—Great excitement before arriving on the Col—"Le diable est mort"—Some difficult rocks—A deserted village—Nine miles through deep snow—We astonish the natives—Fresh projects.

AT eleven o'clock on the morning of the 6th of February, we were already at Lognon. Up there it was difficult to believe oneself in winter, save for the three feet of snow on the roof, and the staircase cut in the snow, leading down to the door. A table and chair were placed in front of the châlet, and I breakfasted in the open air. No furs or wraps were required to keep one warm. The guides were in high spirits, and, after having made the tracks almost to the plateau of the glacier, amused themselves in various ways.

"How difficult it would be," I remarked to Cupelin, "if one were to meet in the mountains with a piece of rock like the walls of the châlet, to ascend it, supposing, of course, that one received no help from any one else."

"Not a bit of it," answered the guide, who at once began to climb it like a monkey. A corniche hung from the roof, but at last, by aid of his ice-axe, he arrived on the top and proceeded to jump down again. Presently I asked, "Could you do that with the tea-things in your hands, and break nothing?"

"To be sure!" And, with the tea-pot in one hand and the cream-jug and cup in the other down he sprang, arriving on his feet, nothing even spilt. Then they teased poor Tourner, who was in an awful fright in case we should insist on his crossing the Col with us. At last it was time to retire for the night.

"We must start at two o'clock," the guides had said. At 2.15 a.m. we set out, and the rest at once began telling Cupelin to "look out for the corniche," and asking "how much the seats cost for the performance? when would his acrobatic feats begin?" &c. One of the guides had gone on in front, and cut away the ledge, making a passage right through it, and a flight of steps down to the plateau below. He now stood at the top of the opening, and begged to "assist Cupelin in descending." What a cold morning it was! We felt warm enough, the exercise prevented our getting chilled, but a little farther on a "crack" was heard in one of the knapsacks. No notice was taken of this till about half-past five o'clock, when the knapsack was opened to get out the wine. Then a bottle of tea was found to be broken in two, and its contents a solid block of ice! The snow was very different to what we had found it on the Chardonnet. It was as soft as snow could be. We made no remark, but one and all feared greatly for the other side. Should the snow there be no better than on the Argentière side, then the excursion would, indeed, be a failure. For, to descend the steep slope just below the summit, with bad snow, was out of the question. The Aiguille Vert saluted us as we passed, by dropping a gigantic sérac almost at our feet. Above the Col Dolent a haze was visible for a few seconds, then it faded away. A mighty avalanche had fallen from a neighbouring peak, and filled the air with its powdered fragments. We toiled up the slopes leading to the Col d'Argentière, while I repeated to myself a sentence in Ball's "Western Alps," apropos of this passage. He says, "The slope on the Argentière side of the Col is not very steep, but the sheer descent on the opposite or east side is positively startling." I was therefore fully prepared to be startled.

At last the summit seemed really near us, and our excitement rose to fever pitch. I hurried till I was out of breath; then had to rest a moment. Should we never get there? it looked so close! But what is that? surely the snow is hardening under our feet. A few steps more, and we were certain that the wind had thoroughly consolidated it. But on the other side? We were now on the top.[1] Nothing however, can be seen of the descent, till one leans over the corniche. I fairly held my breath as Cupelin advanced to the edge. He was there; one glance over and he sprang back, waving his cap and crying, "Le diable est mort! Il est mort! Il est mort!"

"Cupelin, Cupelin, let me look!" I exclaimed. The rest held the rope as I went forward, and in my turn I saw our descent. But I can't say that it startled me, for I did not consider it by any means

[1] The Col d'Argentière is 11,555 feet above the level of the sea.

difficult. This is what I saw. First, all along the top of the Col, the loveliest of corniches, rolled over into the most extravagant shapes. Below it a steep slope of good snow. Then a couloir, not particularly steep. Far down lay the bergschrund, often such a formidable obstacle in summer. It was now bridged over in many places, and everywhere quite narrow. Then came the Glacier de la Neuva. Beyond which, a long moraine, now covered with snow, led to the châlets of La Folie. The view had been a most reassuring one, and I hastily wrote our names to leave on the top, and had a glass of wine. The guides were anxious to begin the descent as soon as possible. I wished to wait a little and enjoy the view. So they left me there, and cut down the slope for twenty minutes. Ball says that the Col "commands a magnificent view." I go further. I thought it the most magnificent view I had ever seen. It is worthily framed, too. One gazes at it through a portal formed on one side by a peak aptly named the Tour Noir, and, on the other, by a few pointed and jagged splinters of rock, beyond which rises the Mont Dolent. Both, when one stands in the middle, seem to descend to the Val Ferret in perpendicular walls of rock. And now for the picture. A perfect sea of mountains throws up their summits across the horizon. A step, it seems, would take one over to the Grand Combin, as he proudly stands in the foreground. Far behind, the peerless Matterhorn, uncovered to "the shoulder," rises against the blue sky. The savage-looking sides of the Dent Blanche come next, and the view to the left ends with the rippling forms of the mountains of the Bernese Oberland. To the right the Alps of Cogne are visible. The valley of Aoste was filled with a smooth white mist, and a fog lingered over the hospice of St. Bernard. Nearer, Mont Dolent pours enormous séracs down his precipitous sides, on to the Glacier de la Neuva; while behind Mont Blanc raises his lofty head above Les Courtes and Les Droites. The Aiguille Vert, too, looks most majestic, as it rises straight out of the basin of the glacier. All too soon the guides returned. First I heard the groaning of their ice-axes, and then the cheerful face of our porter peered through the gap in the corniche, and one by one they emerged on the top. It was then twenty minutes past ten o'clock. I tied myself in my accustomed place (No. 2 descending, No. 3 ascending). We jumped down, and, with axes deeply buried in the snow, pursued our way in the highest spirits.

"Ah!" remarked Auguste, "that corniche just suited my brother."

"Cupelin," I said, "I'm starving."

"Madame, when we've crossed the bergschrund, we will have dinner."

It certainly was better to wait till then, for our present position was not specially designed for picnics, the risk that one of the knapsacks might go to the Val Ferret by a shorter route than that which we proposed to take, being too great. We got into the Grand Couloir, and went down it at express speed, chattering cheerily all the time. Our conversation was made up of self-congratulations and self-conceit. But we were punished for our vanity.

Suddenly Cupelin cried, "We are too low down!"

We ascended a little. It was tiresome work.

"Can't we cross *here?*" I asked (the object was to reach a second couloir beyond some rocks; it led straight down to the glacier).

"We can try," they answered.

It was steep, and the snow had a layer over it of a frozen substance, which, after cutting us, let our feet sink deeply into the soft snow beneath. We were within ten yards of our couloir when some nasty little rocks had to be passed. Michel got over with his usual ingenuity. I tried to follow.

"Hold well, Cupelin; I'm not very secure!"

"All right, madame, I'm secure; don't be afraid.'

A tiny point projected through the snow. I placed my foot carefully on it. But the next step was almost beyond my reach. My gloves were cast aside. I felt through the snow for something to hold, but only smooth surfaces met my grasp. At last I managed to arrive on the second step. My arm could then be thrust through the snow above. The third step was impossible. Michel cleverly turned, and cut me one below in the hard snow. Into it I contrived to drop, a few cuts on my hands remaining as souvenirs of my passage. From there we were once more on the slope, and could advance with ease. In a few minutes the bergschrund was reached; we crossed it, and sat ourselves down on the other side to dine. The sun was bakingly hot, and our faces smarted from the reflection of the snow. We were very hungry, and half an hour was spent there. Then we waded down, through the deep snow, towards the châlets of La Folie. At four o'clock we got to that deserted village. The châlets are not inhabited after the beginning of September, and it seemed forsaken by all humanity. The track of a fox passed through the street, and added to the strange effect. From La Folie the most tiresome part of the day's work began. Nine weary miles lay between us and Orsières, and, until a short distance before the village of Orny, no beaten track was reached.

"Never mind!" said the guides; "it's better than the avalanches after the Chardonnet!"

At 8.45 p.m. we entered the little auberge, and many were the congratulations which we received We left Orsières at six o'clock next morning, and crossed, as before, the Tête Noir. But not in low spirits this time. All the way over the guides laughed and joked each other. At the Tête Noir they declared that it was too difficult for them to pass; that they must go back and return by the Col des Hirondelles, and a hundred other absurdities.

"Have you come from Mont Blanc?" a man inquired, whom we met.

"Yes," answered Cupelin. "We have ascended by Les Aiguilles Grise, and descended by the Glacier de Bruillard."

The man gaped.

"Why did you tell such a fib?" I inquired, when he had passed on.

"Ma foi! It was because people had no business to ask questions."

A little further, and a guide met us. "Where are you coming from?"

"We left Courmayeur this morning, having ascended the Dent du Géant yesterday," was the information which Auguste gave him.

A third was told that we had crossed the Grandes Jorasses. Comte and his sledge were waiting for us at Argentière.

"Well!" he exclaimed, "I did not think it could be done. Now, I suppose you are ready for anything?"

"Certainly!" they answered.

During the drive to Chamonix several plans for the future were discussed. In the following chapter it will be seen which of them was carried into execution.

CHAPTER VI.

A JOURNEY IN THE VALLEYS.

CHAPTER VI.

A JOURNEY IN THE VALLEYS.

Decide for Matterhorn and Monte Rosa—Signor Sella's winter ascent of the former—Ice avalanche on the road to Geneva—At Bonneville—A dexterous porter—Montreux — Incident at Martigny — From Orsières to Liddes—Cupelin manufactures two sledges—Arrival at St. Pierre.

A WEEK'S bad weather followed (bad weather always followed our excursions!). Then came cloudless skies, barometer at "beau-fixe," and every prospect of its remaining there for some time. The month of March would shortly begin, and the spring replace the winter. There was, however, time for one or two more ascents before the former season set in, and I carefully planned a programme for the following week. Its two principal items were the Matterhorn and Monte Rosa. The former had been ascended on the 17th of March, 1882, by Signor Vittorio Sella, accompanied by J. A. Carrel and two other guides of Valtournanche. Leaving Breuil before daylight, they climbed to the summit of the mountain, descending to the upper cabin on the Zermatt side. They got there just as the last remnants of daylight vanished. The night was spent in that neglected hut; the cold was intense, and the interior of the cabin filled with ice and snow. On the following morning this plucky mountaineer and his guides went down to Zermatt. No exceptional difficulties were encountered on the Italian side of the mountain, save that a good deal of work was required on the arête. On the Swiss side, however, the descent was very risky. The slopes, though steeper than on the other face, give much better foot and handhold. All the ledges were, at that season, covered with snow, and the rocks glazed with ice. The northern (or Zermatt) side not being exposed to the sun, the snow was soft and floury. Five hours were consumed in descending from the upper cabin to that built by Mr. Seiler, and now invariably used by tourists in preference to the other. Seeing the great risks a descent on the Swiss side would entail, I determined to ascend from Breuil to the cabin, sleep there, and the next day make the ascent and return to Breuil. But it was understood that, unless the weather was warm and thoroughly settled, the Matterhorn would be abandoned till the following winter, when the new cabin below the Great Tower being finished, no risk of detention by a storm, and the descent rendered impracticable, could occur. As for Monte Rosa, it had never before been ascended in winter, and, unless beaten by bad weather, we were sure to do it. The ascent is not a difficult one; it is almost as easy as that of Mont Blanc, though longer and very tiresome.

"There certainly is one advantage at this season," I remarked to Cupelin; "we need fear no rivals in the field."

"Not much chance of meeting another caravan on Monte Rosa, I think," said my guide.

"Then, Cupelin," I continued, "if this weather lasts, we will do the Matterhorn first, and afterwards Monte Rosa."

"And when will madame start?" he asked.

"I really can't cross that odious Tête Noir again," I answered; "but I shall leave this afternoon for Geneva, and you can all meet me at Martigny; I don't want to cross a Col, as I shall require all my strength for our two ascents. Besides, Mademoiselle A. goes with me to our different headquarters, and you know that she cannot walk much in the mountains."

"Madame is right," replied Cupelin; "we shall be waiting at Martigny railway station with a carriage for St. Pierre when you and mademoiselle arrive there."

We left that afternoon in the most perfect weather which it is possible to imagine. Not a cloud was to be seen on the sky. The air was still and warm; a real summer's day it seemed to us. The sun shone brightly and the heat of the glowing orb melted the glistening icicles which fringed the rocks. In passing that part of the road which runs close along a high wall of rock, a whizzing sound was heard over our heads. We looked up. An enormous block of ice was flying down towards us. Before a word could be uttered it had struck the edge of the carriage on A.'s side, and broke into a thousand fragments. Our driver clutched his head with both hands, crying, " Oh, malheur! I thought it was coming upon my hat. Never was I so frightened in my life! No, never, never!"

"Well, it's all right now," said A., rather scornfully; "it was about an inch from my shoulder, and I was afraid that it would fall on the horses."

"The horses!" exclaimed the valiant driver; "better a thousand times that it should smash, knock down the horses, than hurt *me!*"

Poor man, his plaintive expression made us laugh for the next mile. That night we spent at Bonneville. The hotel was crowded, as there had been a funeral in the morning, and the guests had come from Paris, Lyons, and other remote parts of France. They had breakfast next day at the same hour as ourselves, and, to judge by the amount of hot rolls, eggs, and coffee which they consumed, their feelings must have been too deep to permit them to eat the day before, or else their share in the will was a large one. They crowded the three diligences which started for Geneva, but fortunately we had engaged two outside places the evening before, and mounted aloft in triumph, while the others were crammed into the stuffy interior. One rather portly monsieur demurred, whereupon the conductor cried, "Will any lady go inside to oblige a gentleman?" No response followed, and the discontented one was packed beneath us.

A thick fog covered all the surrounding hills as we started, but gradually cleared off, and, when we got to Geneva at half-past eleven o'clock, the day was as fine a one as could be desired. As fine, yes. But what a different quality of fineness to that which we had left 2000 feet higher. None of those clear, sharp outlines; none of that brightly glittering snow; but a hazy softness of form, and at sunset a crimson ball of fire which sunk beyond the lake. Can such a climate be healthy? For some, perhaps; but when I find myself in a lake district I either shiver from the damp, or stifle from the want of air. The diligence stopped near the Quai du Mont Blanc. We got down, and I asked for a porter to carry our baggage as far as the Hôtel Suisse. A ragged individual volunteered. He gazed vaguely at the rope, helplessly at the knapsack, and my ice-axe, and A——'s stick completely baffled him. He then tried to load himself. The stick went over one shoulder, with the knapsack hung to it, the ice-axe over the other, and A——'s bundle suspended to its point. The rope still seemed a stumbling-block, but he balanced it somewhere and started. Before he had gone two minutes he had managed to drop everything in the very middle of the thoroughfare. A crowd gathered round. I was sorely perplexed between the desire to rescue my property and the strong dislike of owning our imbecile porter. The conductor came to the rescue With one swoop he had lifted up the rope, hung it round the neck of the employé, put the knapsack on his back, and the packet in one hand, the stick and axe in the other. The crowd giggled, and we pursued our way. Many were the anxious glances I cast behind, but the porter followed like an automaton, and we arrived without accident at the doors of the hotel. I received many congratulations from the worthy landlady regarding my improved appearance.

"Ah, but madame looks now the picture of health!" she exclaimed. "Did I not say that the mountain air is the best medicine?"

Breakfast was partaken of, and the excellent cuisine of that most comfortable hotel duly appreciated. We left by an afternoon train for Montreux. Why will the Swiss railway companies heat their carriages to such an extent, regardless of the outside temperature? On a day when the thermometer marks about sixty degrees of heat, the stoves and foot-warmers and invariably closed windows are brought into service, just the same as during the most bitter cold. At Montreux we found friends, one of the best hotels in Switzerland (Hôtel Monney), and a climate which seemed tropical after the fresh air of Chamonix. A very pleasant evening was spent there, and many warnings received from kind Mrs. C., whose fear of the mountains caused her real uneasiness when I announced my intention of ascending the Matterhorn a few days later. A good night's rest and a comfortable room were most acceptable, and eleven o'clock next day found us at Martigny. On the platform were our three retainers, and a carriage waited outside. We got in and drove off towards Orsières and St. Pierre. Our cocher was an old man whom we had employed on a former occasion when a rather amusing incident occurred.

It was the 1st of November. We had crossed the Col du Tour, and intended to ascend the Dent du Midi next day from Martigny. It would have been more convenient to do so from Vernayaz, but I imagined, somehow, that the hotel there, the Hôtel Gorges de Trient, was closed in winter. Therefore I determined to spend the night at the Hôtel Mont-Blanc (such a good hotel) at Martigny. On arriving there, the Hôtel Mont-Blanc was shut. I went accordingly to another, had dinner, and afterwards ordered the provisions for the following day. I wished to leave at 2 a.m. Cupelin told the proprietor that the guides would require nothing before leaving, and that I should only want a cup of tea. The answer which he received was, "Do you think that I shall trouble myself to make a cup of tea at two o'clock in the morning?" Cupelin made no reply, but reported the conversation to me, adding, "I hear that the hotel at Vernayaz is open."

"Please to order a carriage, pay the bill, put in the knapsacks, and let us leave at once," I said.

In a quarter of an hour we drove off.

"How did you manage so quickly?" I asked Cupelin.

"Madame, I went to the nearest café, and there I saw our driver. I inquired, 'Do you know of any one who will drive us at once to Vernayaz?'

'Yes,' answered the man. 'Where are you at present?'

"I mentioned the name of our inn.

"'Oh, if it's to conduct a party from there to Vernayaz, I'm the man.'

"'Why?'

"'Ah! I know the landlord. A selfish creature, who will have all for himself and nothing for anybody else.'"

How we rattled along the piece of road leading from Martigny to Vernayaz, surprising the inmates of the Hôtel Gorges de Trient, who certainly did not expect visitors at that hour. Very different was the behaviour of the host of that comfortable hotel. His wife was up at 1 a.m. next morning getting my breakfast, and looking as energetic and contented as if it were twelve hours later.

But to go back to our drive to Orsières. A⸺'s spirits were bubbling over; it was her first visit to Switzerland, and everything seemed delightful. The road was in ruts, and inches deep in mud, and it was long before we at last clattered along the stony streets of Orsières. We breakfasted there, and the driver inquired if the carriage could go as far as St. Pierre. He was told that it was impossible to get beyond Liddes, but that there we should find sledges. After an hour's halt, we left. Reader, if ever you go to Orsières, remember two things: First, that the Hôtel des Alpes is much better than it looks; and secondly, that the cream there is something not to be forgotten. Soon after starting, A—— exclaimed,—

"May I ride one of the horses?"

"No!"

"Then may I drive?"

"Ask the cocher."

He did not mind, and my young friend took the reins, and kept them till we got to Liddes. The driver amused us greatly by some of his stories. It appeared that he was also a guide, and had mules, besides, for crossing the Col de Balme and other excursions. Once he was engaged to drive two English girls over to Chamonix by the Tête Noir. When the carriage came to the door they cried,—

"Those horses are too good to drive. Get two saddles, and we will ride them."

He did so, and the young ladies, on being mounted, trotted off at the rate of ten miles an hour.

"They went *so* and *so*," said our driver, bumping himself up and down on the seat. "I never saw any lady ride so before, and I did not pick them up for two hours. They got to Chamonix two hours before me, though I drove from Argentière."

Another description of a family with whom he travelled made us laugh.

"There were two *miss*," he said, "and a great, tall, black servant. He never said a word, but one day, when we spoke to him, he just turned back his coat and showed us what he had in his pockets. Madame, it is the truth which I tell you. He had in one pocket three revolvers, and in the other five long knives!"

One more anecdote — this time a really curious example of the sagacity of animals. Our driver had accompanied three ladies over the Col de Bonhomme. A fearful storm came on. Snow fell heavily. The path was lost. One of the ladies fainted, and another was nearly frozen. They wandered about for hours, our cocher carrying the lady who was insensible. At last the idea of letting the mules try and find the way, occurred to one of the party. The animals were allowed to choose any direction they wished, and before long they actually discovered the path.

We arrived at Liddes just as it began to get dusk. The streets were slippery with ice, and cut up into ruts. Driving through them was no easy matter, but A—— would not abandon her post, and the peasants flocked out in troops to gaze at such a curiosity as a party of tourists in winter. We asked if they could give us two sledges.

"Sledges, no." There was not one to be had.

"Not one of any kind?" asked Cupelin.

"Only this!" said a bystander, producing a sort of wooden frame, consisting of two long pieces of wood and two short ones, the latter fastened across the former.

"Then we must manufacture two sledges," said Cupelin.

He asked for wood, hammer, and nails, and set to work, the whole population of Liddes watching the operation with the greatest interest. The cushions of the carriage were brought into requisition, and, after half an hour or so, two very respectable little sledges were turned out. One of the horses was harnessed to each, and we prepared to start. Myself, the driver, and Auguste Cupelin occupied the first; and A—— drove Edouard Cupelin and the porter in the second. For some time all went well. The great difficulty had been in fastening the shafts to the animals. The harness had been hooked on to them by a bit of wood; but before going very far it smashed. A hole through the shaft, and a piece of string, was suggested. For this purpose nothing was forthcoming but our rope or a boot-lace; the latter was chosen, and we proceeded. Shortly before arriving at St. Pierre, the road got so bad that Cupelin advised A—— to give him the reins. She declined, so he mounted the horse, and remained in that position till we entered the town.

We had dinner and retired early, for the start next day was fixed for 6 a.m. We were to cross the St. Bernard, and get to Chatillon the same evening. I was really curious to see the celebrated hospice in winter, and will keep my account of our passage for the next chapter.

CHAPTER VII.

THE GRAND ST. BERNARD IN WINTER.

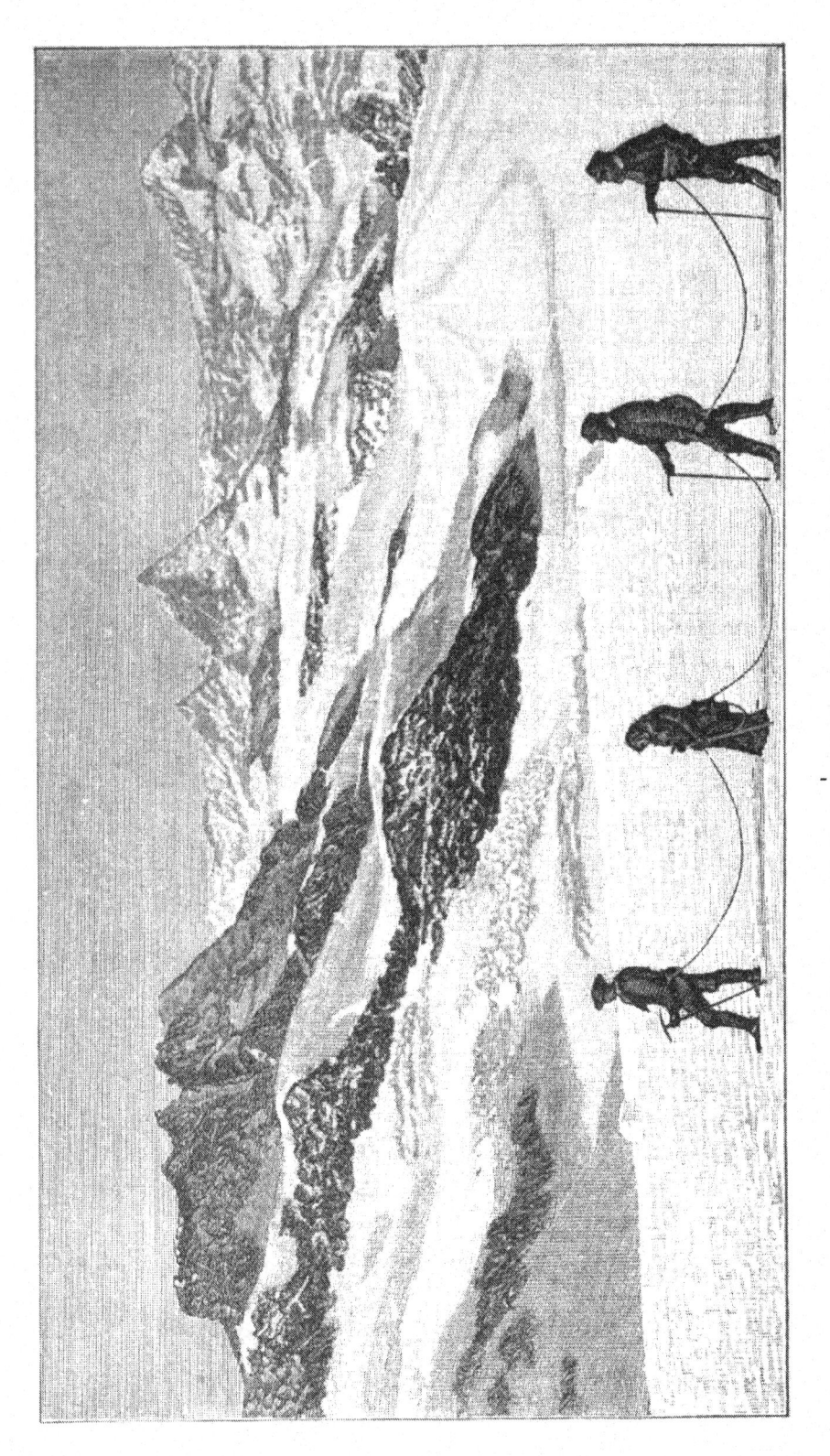

Directly after having left the highest point which we had attained.

Page 113.

CHAPTER VII.

THE GRAND ST. BERNARD IN WINTER.

Signs of bad weather—A ferocious dog—The monks in winter costume—I fail to discover the entrance to the hospice—A new dish—An amusing descent—" La glissade de Madame "—The Italian custom-house—Cupelin's fourteen pockets—A runaway mule—No carriages at Aoste—The heat of the valley—Arrival at Chatillon—Disastrous tidings.

NEXT morning (March 1), at dawn, we assembled at the door of the Hôtel Déjeuner de Napoléon. How different it was to my last start for the hospice on that cold and windy evening some three weeks before. The snow was hard, and we walked briskly on the well-marked track. An hour and a quarter sufficed for us to reach the Cantine of Proz, but alas! alas! it sufficed also for many angry-looking clouds to cover the sky which had been so clear an hour before. If snow should fall and spoil our beloved Matterhorn! How anxious I felt as we wended our way onwards and glanced from time to time at the thickly-gathering mists. The sky puzzled me. To the north were layers of indigo-coloured clouds and a single streak of the palest blue above the horizon. The wind seemed furious in the upper regions, but it was from the north, and how bad weather could prevail with a north wind was what I could not imagine.

"We won't pay any attention to the weather," said the guides; "let us get to Valtournanche, and then we will see what we can do."

"Moi, j'ai bonne espérance," remarked Cupelin.

About half-way between the Cantine and the hospice, a party in the act of descending came in sight; an enormous dog marched in front. It turned out to be five of the monks who were going down with provisions and wine to the refuge where persons overcome by the cold and fatigue take shelter. The dog was by no means friendly, and rushed towards me, as I headed our caravan, growling like thunder. I valiantly brandished my ice-axe in his face, but he did not take the hint and retire. On the contrary, he seemed ready to fly at me, and I ignominiously sought a safer place behind the broad back of my guide. The animal quieted down, however, after a few words from the monks. They carried a pocket-handkerchief-full of provisions and several flasks of wine. They offered us some of the latter, and we accepted, and found it excellent. And now, without disrespect to the good monks, let me describe their costume; for I am sure that the summer tourist has never seen the holy fathers attired in anything so unclerical. Top-boots, or gaiters, snuff-coloured knickerbockers, short coats, woollen gloves, and head-gear varying from red foulards to fur caps. They told us that they did not think badly of the weather, and we continued our way with lighter hearts, hoping that they might be right. At a quarter to ten we arrived in front of the hospice. I looked for the front door, and not seeing it, prepared to go round to the other side of the building.

"This way, madame," called Cupelin.

He was just entering a small and low portal, and I could not understand why we were to go in that way.

"How different to the summer," he said, as I came up.

Suddenly the fact dawned upon me that the great depth of snow was the reason for our apparent change of route, and that the same entrance which in summer is approached by seven or eight steps upwards, is now attained by three steps downwards. A troop of dogs came rushing to meet us as we entered, and did not seem more amiable than their companion whose acquaintance we had made an half hour before. No monks were to be seen till Cupelin gave the great bell a tug which made it give forth a sound that echoed throughout all the length of the galleries. Then the director of the monastery appeared and welcomed us with his usual hospitality. Dinner was quickly prepared, and very hungry we were. First came soup, then fish cooked with cheese and eggs, and finally a dish of curious little black creatures, quite new both to A—— and myself. We had eaten about half of them when A—— suddenly put down her knife and fork, and exclaimed,—

"I know what they are!"

"Do you?" I said. "What are they, then?"

"I don't like to tell you; you won't eat any more if I do," she answered.

"I don't mind as long as they taste good," I replied.

"Well" said A——, "I think that they're—slugs."

I did *not* eat any more.

Presently the monk returned, and asked about our travels since my last visit there. Afterwards he showed A—— the library and chapel, and then it was time to start. The weather had greatly improved; large patches of blue were to be seen all over the sky. We tramped across the lake, now a smooth plateau of snow, and then came a little excitement, for we had to descend the ropes. Those who have visited the Hospice of St. Bernard in summer will, no doubt, remember that, when approaching it from the Italian side, and just before getting to the top of the pass, a steep slope has to be ascended. To mount this, the mule-path makes a wide détour, and reaches the top by several zigzags. In winter the path is entirely obliterated, and a smooth and steep slope of snow replaces the grass and stones. Straight down this slope are placed long poles, and a rope passes from one to the other. It was down this rope that we proceeded to go. Cupelin and Michel were in front, I came next, and A—— and Auguste behind.

"Take care of mademoiselle, you need pay no attention to me," I cried.

I put my arm over the rope, and slid rapidly from post to post. A—— got on capitally, and would not let Auguste help her, so he passed on in front, and, by the time I had finished the last post but two, was already halfway down the couloir. The couloir was rather steep, but a standing glissade ought to take one down it beautifully; so I left my post, crossed to the middle, and prepared for a good slide. I was in the act of arranging my axe when my feet slipped from under me, and off I went down the couloir, on the hard snow, like an express train.

"Stop me!" I cried to Auguste, though I felt sure that he could not on such snow, and that I should only knock him over too. He dared not put in his ice-axe, I might have cut myself with it, and, as I shot up against him, he too fell, and down we both slid at the rate of sixty miles an hour. I managed to glance below, and saw that the plateau was not far distant. The others were laughing heartily at our rapid descent, as we arrived there; and A—— far from being discouraged, was quite ready to follow our example. "La glissade de madame," became quite as much a proverb as Cupelin's corniche or Auguste's crevasse. There was a good track, but the snow lower down was soft, and made more so by the hot sun which shone over our heads. For by this time every cloud had vanished, and the fine weather seemed quite to have returned. At St. Rémy is the Italian custom-house, and as we passed, one of the officials called out,—

"The Douane. Please to come in for the examination of your luggage."

"Not I," said Cupelin; "if you want to look at our knapsacks, you had better come to the hotel."

However, the whole force of three charged down upon us, and we were obliged to follow them. Everything was opened. A cardboard box containing chocolate excited their curiosity in my knapsack.

"What is that?"

"Chocolate."

"No! it's tobacco."

"Then taste it."

He did so, and restored it to me with a growl. A potted tongue was turned over and over.

"Tongue, what does that mean?"

"Langue," I answered.

"Are you sure that it is not the English for *tabac?*" we heard them inquire of each other.

Every article was taken out, the inside even of the wine-gourds seemed to them suspicious. At last they had finished, but Cupelin, whom this examination had provoked beyond measure, was determined to have his little revenge.

"Is that the way you do your work?" he exclaimed; "why, you've not examined our pockets yet, you will have the goodness to begin with mine; I have fourteen." Deliberately he began to empty them, one by one, till he came to a small packet of tobacco. "I suppose that much is allowed?" said he. The custom-house officers seized on his little store, weighed it, took one half, and returned the other to him. "Que j'étais bête de les laisser voir!" grumbled poor Cupelin.

A short halt was made at the hotel while a carriage was got ready. A curious vehicle it turned out to be, totally destitute of springs, and drawn by a very frisky mule. In descending the zigzags a little beyond St. Rémy a sledge met us. The guides and coachman helped to lift it past, our conveyance meanwhile drawn up by the railings. I suppose that something startled our animal, for in a second he started off down the hill at a gallop. The men clung on behind like leeches, and presently managed to stop the creature, just as we came to the end of the zigzag. As they got up I made the remark which we had several occasions afterwards to find so true: "The greatest dangers are in the valleys, on the roads, and not in the mountains!"

What a road that was! Ruts, stones, blocks of ice, in a word, every evil thing seemed combined on that highway. And then to jolt over it all in a cart without springs! For me it was not so bad, I was accustomed to most kinds of locomotion of a primitive order, but poor A—— looked very woeful, and great was her joy when Aoste at length was seen below. What a change to descend to that valley as it lay basking in the sunshine, and with green fields, looking hardly more like winter than when I last visited it in August. Our rickety conveyance put us down at the Hôtel du Mont-Blanc. There, things certainly were different. No bustling landlady and busy waiters, but silence and not a living soul to be seen. We knocked, we called, but to no effect. Finally I departed upstairs to search for some human beings, and Cupelin descended to the lower regions. He was the more successful of the two, and unearthed the landlady in the kitchen.

"Have you got a carriage?" he asked, as soon as he saw her.

"A carriage? yes. You will want it—when? Not too early to-morrow, I hope, as the horses are in the country."

"To-morrow!" exclaimed Cupelin; "but we want it in five minutes!"

"I am really very sorry," said the landlady, "but I'm sure you won't be able to find a carriage in Aoste before to-morrow."

"Well, I shall try, at any rate," he answered, and forthwith strode off, all the inhabitants staring after the tall figure in the gaiters. In five minutes he returned, a carriage following close behind, our baggage was swept into it, some wine and bread taken from the hotel, and we were once more en route. It was then ten minutes past five, and we wished to reach Chatillon as early as possible. Clouds of dust enveloped us as we drove along, and the stuffiness was intense. We dined during the journey, and at half-past seven crossed the picturesque bridge leading to the hotel. A—— and I had supper, and then sent for the guides to arrange for the start next morning. They came to speak to us in the passage, and their faces wore an unusually grave aspect. What could be the matter?

"Cupelin, I'm sure there is some bad news," I said.

"Madame," he answered, "I have just heard something which has provoked me very much."

"But what is it?"

"I fear that we have lost Monte Rosa."

"You don't mean to say that some one else has done it!" I exclaimed.

"Not yet," he answered; "but Signor Sella passed here yesterday, and is to ascend Monte Rosa to-morrow if the weather is fine."

"Oh, how I hope it will not be fine then," I could not help thinking. I fancy that Cupelin read my thoughts, for he remarked,—

"If it is not fine they can't do it; but then, if the weather is bad, we too shall miss our course."

"Well," I said, "we cannot get there first, if he starts to-morrow morning, and I see nothing for us to do but to go up early to Breuil."

"Where is Signor Sella now?" I asked the landlord.

"At the Riffel," he answered.

"Cupelin, turn over every plan you can think of to outwit them," I said. "I will do the same, and to-morrow we will compare notes."

"Madame, if they are to be outwitted, we will do it," he replied.

The mules for A—— and myself were then

ordered for 6 a.m., and we retired to our rooms. All night I dreamt that we were going up Monte Rosa, and that an Italian caravan, whose tracks we were following, waited calmly to receive us at the top.

CHAPTER VIII.

CHATILLON TO VALTOURNANCHE.

CHAPTER VIII.

CHATILLON TO VALTOURNANCHE.

Jean-Antoine Carrel—Plans to outwit the Italian caravan—A true mountaineer—The weather continues to get worse—Lack of provisions at Valtournanche—The return of the enemy.

As the clock struck six next day we mounted our mules, and were soon winding along the valley leading to Valtournanche. The peasants looked wondrously astonished to see "les Anglaises" at that season, and stared hard as we passed. Presently a figure was seen racing down the road.

"Ah, there is our man!" cried Cupelin.

"Who is it?" I asked.

"Jean-Antoine," he replied.

This was then the famous Carrel of whom I had read so much, who had first stormed the Matterhorn from the Italian side, who had been up Chimborazo,[1] who had crossed the Matterhorn with Signor Sella last winter, and who had been spoken of by Mr. Whymper as the finest rock-climber he had ever seen. I looked at him with something approaching to awe. Cupelin, however, hailed him very unceremoniously.

"Hi! Carrel! We want two porters for to-morrow to go to the cabin on the Matterhorn. Will you and your eldest son come?"

"Yes, *I* will come, but my eldest son is away with his mother. However, if my second son will do instead, I will take him."

"Is he sure?"

"Yes, you can rely on him."

"Good, come up to Breuil at once, then."

[1] In the Andes, 21,421 feet above the level of the sea, ascended by Mr. Whymper, January 4th, 1880, accompanied by the guides Jean-Antoine and Louis Carrel.

"I shall be there almost as soon as you; but I must first go into Chatillon for half an hour."

"Very well; only don't go to a café, but do what you have to do, and follow us as quickly as possible."

"Bien; au revoir."

"He is older than I thought," I remarked to Cupelin, "but he is a resolute-looking man, and must have been a first-rate guide in his time."

By this time the weather had undergone very much the same kind of change which had taken place the day before while we were passing the St. Bernard. All the mountains were concealed by mist, and the wind above was high.

"I don't think that they can have gone up to-day," remarked Cupelin ("they," of course, referred to Signor Sella and his guides).

"I don't know," I answered; "perhaps, if they started very early from the Riffel they may have done it."

"Has madame thought of a plan in case they have not got there?" inquired my guide.

"Yes," I said; "but I am afraid you will think it hardly practicable; it is as follows. If this weather continues we dare not try the Matterhorn, for which two and perhaps three fine warm days are an absolute necessity. For Monte Rosa one good day will suffice, and I propose that, should no change for the better take place in the weather, we leave Breuil to-night at midnight for the Col St. Théodule. On arriving there we can see whether there are tracks for Monte Rosa or not. If there should be, we will amuse ourselves by ascending the Breithorn. If, however, no traces are visible, we shall at once descend to Zermatt, take our provisions from there, and start for Monte Rosa between nine and ten o'clock the same evening. We shall pass the Riffel, and go straight towards our work. How I should like to see the faces of the Italians when they turn out a little later and find their tracks already made for them!"

"Madame, I had the very same idea," replied Cupelin; " it is the only way of preventing the others from ascending Monte Rosa for the first time in winter."

I am afraid that our feelings towards " the others" were the reverse of charitable that morning as we discussed our scheme and watched the weather with malicious satisfaction. It was evidently not snowing in the heights, therefore these clouds would not injure the Matterhorn. Certainly circumstances seemed to smile on us. Still we were very uneasy in case, after all, the ascension might have taken place already, or might succeed the next day. It was useless to talk over the question any longer, we could only wait and see, "and my opinion," added Cupelin, "is, that we shall meet them coming back, having tried the mountain and been beaten by the weather." This subject dismissed for the present, the guides exerted themselves to amuse us and each other, and make the time pass as pleasantly as they could.

"Madame, do you see that man in front? how he stares at us! I am going to say something to him."

Accordingly, with a smiling countenance, our guide advanced, holding out his hand. The man looked surprised, and Cupelin exclaimed,—

"Don't you know me?"

"No! I don't think I do," answered the other.

"Why," said Cupelin, "we had a glass of wine together at Aoste two years ago."

"Yes, yes; I remember now," cried the man.

"You see," remarked Cupelin, "your face is such a striking one that I remembered it *à l'instant même*, but as for me, I'm so ordinary-looking that I don't wonder you forgot me."

They once more shook hands warmly. When we had gone a little farther, I said,—

"I suppose you never saw that man before, did you?"

"Never in my life, madame."

Then he chaffed the poor old man who led my

mule. This individual was short and stumpy. His shoulders were up to his ears, and his long hair gave him a very uncanny look.

"Can you tell me, my good man," began Cupelin, with the utmost gravity, "if the mule-path up the Matterhorn is almost completed?"

"Not that I know of," was the answer.

"Because," continued my guide, "we heard at Chamonix that it was finished as far as the cabin, but we did not believe it."

"No," said the man; "I don't think that they are making one, but so many wonderful things have been done since my time that I can't be sure."

"Have *you* ever ascended the Matterhorn," asked Cupelin.

"Yes."

"And is it difficult?"

"No, not very."

"Do you think that *I* could get there?" inquired the gigantic Frenchman.

"Yes, I think you could," answered the old man.

"We must respect the old," said Cupelin in a loud tone, turning to me, " and especially when one can see so much capacity for great things left. Now, that is what I call a mountaineer," he remarked, pointing down to the flowing locks.

A peasant carrying an enormous spade passed presently.

"How much will you take for that spade?" inquired Cupelin.

"Do you want to buy it?" asked the peasant.

"Yes, to shovel out the snow on the cabin of the Matterhorn. I'll give you a franc."

The man gaped, but the idea of being joked did not occur to him.

With these and many other absurdities, crowned by our guide picking up a looking-glass which had fallen from the pocket of our companion with the flowing hair, the time was wiled away, and Valtournanche appeared in front of us, perched

against the opposite hill. We went to the hotel
and there more news awaited us. Signor Sella, it
appeared, was not at the Riffel, but at the hut on
the Col St. Théodule! Therefore, if he had made
the ascent, he would be back that evening at Valtournanche. If not, his guides would be forced to
descend for more provisions. Patience! we should
soon know all. Our next move was to inquire as
to the resources of the village as far as fresh meat
was concerned.

"We have some veal," the girl informed us.

"How much?"

"Two cutlets."

"Two cutlets for five people for three days?"

"Oh, but we have salt meat also."

This was a cheerful prospect! I told Cupelin to
do the best he could. Fortunately our own stores
contained two pots of preserved beef, and I had
hopes of finding a chicken in the village. The
clouds still hung low in the valley and the baro-

meter continued to descend. Really, it was too bad to have come all this way and then find weather which might prevent any excursions from being accomplished. A—— and I were having breakfast off the afore-mentioned two cutlets, when some one knocked at the door.

"Come in!"

Cupelin appeared, with a look of satisfaction on his face.

"Well?"

"Madame, it is as I said; Signor Sella and his party have come back."

CHAPTER IX.

COL ST. THÉODULE.

CHAPTER IX.

COL ST. THÉODULE.

Signor Sella—We decide to ascend Monte Rosa together—Cupelin finds a chicken—Start for Breuil—The Matterhorn—Aspect of the hut—Difficulty in getting in—The shortest passage of the Matterhorn—Strange dishes—*En route* for Monte Rosa.

AND it was a fact! The unsuccessful ones were at that moment in the hotel.

"We've got them this time!" chuckled my guide.

"I will see Signor Sella presently," I said, "and he will tell us the reason of his return, and I am sure will also give us some particulars of his ascent of the Matterhorn last winter."

Cupelin then retired, but came back in a few minutes with a boot in his hand.

"What is that?" I asked.

"One of the Signor's boots," replied my guide.

"But why do you bring it here?" I inquired.

"Because, madame, I considered it remarkable," he answered, exhibiting the heel, which was garnished with a steel horse-shoe and five long ice-nails. "I would not take a thousand francs and go up a mountain in that!" said Cupelin.

However, as Signor Sella told us afterwards that it was really very comfortable, perhaps the use or otherwise of the appliance is merely a matter of taste, though I still feel inclined to agree with my guide.

In half an hour or so Signor Sella appeared, and was most kind in giving us every information on the different subjects for which we required it. He told us that he had spent two nights at a châlet at Breuil, intending to move up to the hut on the Col St. Théodule when the weather improved. Their provisions had now run short, and they had come down to Valtournanche to replenish their stores.

"And when shall you return to the attack?" I asked.

"We start for the St. Théodule this evening," he answered.

"You do not, then, consider the weather hopeless?" I inquired.

"No," he replied, "I think that it will improve, and we shall be able to judge better after sunset."

"Then you will ascend Monte Rosa the day after to-morrow," I remarked.

"Yes, if the weather is fine," was the answer.

"Then," said the unabashed Cupelin, "we will assist monsieur to make the tracks. We shall be ready to leave this evening for the St. Théodule at the same hour as monsieur."

"Monsieur" was polite enough to say that this

arrangement would give him much pleasure, but I feared that my walking powers were greatly inferior to his. However, he assured me that he never walked fast, that the plan was a convenient one for both parties, and finally it was decided as my guide had suggested. Then once more came the question of provisions. Signor Sella inquired if there was any fresh meat, and was informed that there *had* been two veal cutlets, but that madame and mademoiselle, &c., &c. He, too, had some tins of potted meat and also half a chicken. I mentioned my hopes of finding another, but he was doubtful, the good people of Valtournanche don't like selling their poultry.

"Cupelin, you must get me a chicken," I said.

"Madame, I will go all through the village, and if I can't buy one, why—I will steal one; madame shall have something to eat."

Needless to say that as with him the "will" was always a strong one, the "way" was invariably found, and the chicken was bought, plucked, and cooked in due course of time. Dinner (a milky sort of soup and salted veal) was partaken of at six o'clock, and by that time all clouds had disappeared from the sky, thanks to the persistence of the north wind. Signor Sella thought that 3 a.m. would be early enough to start, and the proprietor of the hotel at Breuil was to accompany us as far as that village. We were to breakfast and to take our supply of wine from there. Every one retired early, and at 2.30 we assembled once more in the salle-à-manger for coffee, &c., before starting. The moon shone clearly over the valley, and the sky was free from all haze. The air was colder than it had been the day before, and this we thought a good sign. Jean-Antoine was to come with us to the Col, as porter, and also Signor Sella's servant, who has accompanied his master in every ascent (with the exception of the winter ones) which he has made. A long string we formed as we filed along, the proprietor of Breuil and a comrade bringing up the rear. The walk over such hard crisp snow was really a charming one, and A—— arrived at Breuil as fresh as when she left Valtournanche. We were hungry, and devoured quantities of bread-and-butter—about the only eatable thing we could get. A large tin of turtle-soup, made by ourselves some five days before, was excellent, and proved more useful during our excursion than anything else. A roaring fire burnt merrily on the hearth, but we could not remain long as we wanted to get to the Col as early as possible. The knapsacks were shouldered and we once more started upwards. The day was lovely. Not a cloud concealed the distant mountains clothed in snow down to their very feet. The superb pyramid to our left stood up sharply and grandly against the sky. When the Matterhorn comes into the picture description is useless, for no one who has gazed on its unrivalled form can ever forget the impression the first sight of it gave him, and those who have not seen it cannot realize by mere word-painting, the magnificence of this unique specimen of nature's highest efforts. It was the first time that I had ever been near to the king of mountains, and I could hardly advance a step without turning to look. I walked on in front, and arrived alone half an hour below the summit of the Col. Then I sat down and had another good gaze at the Matterhorn. Presently the others joined me, and soon we arrived at the cabin.[1] A—— and Auguste Cupelin got there about two hours later. The little hut had been broken into by smugglers, and the windows were smashed. The interior was filled with snow, and the door would not open. The guides managed to scramble in somehow, but whether they did so through the windows or down the chimney I could not discover. Cartloads of snow were thrown out by the window, and after

[1] The Col St. Théodule is 10,899 feet above sea level.

an hour's work they got the place clear. Then the door had to be opened, but it was easier said than done, the keyhole was blocked with ice.

"Ma foi," said Cupelin, "I think that we had better warm the key over madame's spirit-lamp."

At last the opening of the door was accomplished, and we went in. The lighting of the fire was almost as great a business as it had been in January at the Grands Mulets. By the time A—— arrived, the hut was already in some kind of order; chairs and cooking utensils had been rooted out by Carrel, and some soup was simmering on the stove.

Signor Sella's guides were J. B. Bic, and Joseph Marquinaz—Carrel and the former, it will be remembered, made the first ascent of the Matterhorn from the Italian side. Joseph Marquinaz made the first ascent of the Dent du Géant; there was also a porter. These men were all excellent guides, but on snow and ice there is no doubt that Edouard

Cupelin was their superior—and he is, without exception,[2] the very best guide I know. The afternoon passed pleasantly enough. Every one had some break-neck story to relate, and my guides gave an account of our passage of the Col du Tacul, which was certainly startling—even to me who had been there.

"The last part was *so*," said Cupelin, standing his ice-axe bolt upright on the floor, "and if you fell you would have gone *so!*" passing his hand down it in a suggestive manner till he came to the boards, supposed, no doubt, to represent the Glacier de Léchaud.

"Have you ever ascended the Matterhorn?" Signor Sella asked him.

"Yes, sir, several times" ("We all have," said my guides); "and I think that we crossed it in a shorter time than it has been done before or since."

[2] My second guide, A. Cupelin, made the second ascent of this mountain with Mr. Graham and one of the Payots. On this occasion the highest point was attained for the first time.

"Really! and how long did you take?"

"We left Zermatt at 1 a.m., and got to Breuil at 5 p.m. I had two English gentlemen with me. When we arrived at the ropes they said,—

"'We are sailors, you need pay no more attention to us.'

"And down they scrambled, like two monkeys."

It is wonderful what peculiar kinds of dishes guides fabricate, when they do their own cooking. A marvellous kind of soup, made out of bread and cheese boiled in water, seemed very popular; and numerous other vegetable compounds were manufactured. At 7 p.m. mattresses were spread over the floor, and each one retired to rest, if not to sleep. A—— dozed off in five minutes, and did not wake till we were getting ready to start. I sat up over the fire and read till midnight. Then a solemn voice proclaimed, "Time to get ready," and a general bustle ensued. I made soup, Signor Sella had a cup of coffee; the knapsacks were packed, gaiters and thick boots put on, our heads enveloped in every queer head-gear possible, and the ropes uncoiled. Signor Sella had named 1 a.m. for the start, and I was determined that my caravan should be ready to leave exactly at the appointed time. It wanted two minutes to one, so I tied up my men, and put the last touches to our preparations. The Italian guides seemed still to be dawdling about, though their master was ready.

"They want us to go in front," whispered Cupelin.

The lanterns were lighted, and the two parties filed out, we first, and the Italians behind.

CHAPTER X.

MONTE ROSA.

CHAPTER X.

MONTE ROSA.

Descent of a sérac—The Italian guides don't like it—A tiresome plateau—Intense cold—A violent hurricane—Signor Sella's guides refuse to continue—My nose gets frost-bitten—We turn back—We are photographed—We say good-bye to the others—Our reasons for leaving the Matterhorn alone—Arrival at Zermatt—Biner—A——comes down—Our sledge overturned—We miss the train at Visp—The Salvan *versus* the Tête Noir—Return to Chamonix.

"You had better keep along the rocks to your right," called out Bic to our leader.[1]

[1] Cupelin was first; then Auguste, myself, and Michel. This was always our order in ascending. On leaving the Col an hour's descent must first be made; then there is a plateau; and then the ascent begins. Expecting no difficulties, we had arranged ourselves for the ascent, so as not to have the trouble of changing later on.

"I was going to take the ordinary route round to the left," answered Cupelin.

"The other is shorter, we have passed it a hundred times," responded the other.

"Good! I don't know it, but if you do, it's all right. Are you sure that there are no séracs or crevasses?"

"Quite sure!" answered the Italian guides.

They directed us from behind, and we walked quickly for an hour. Then Cupelin stopped.

"What is the matter?" I asked, as I saw him peering forwards with the lantern.

"Sérac, madame."

We were on the top of one, and there seemed to be plenty of gaping crevasses below. The others suggested returning and taking the other passage —"And losing an hour," grumbled Cupelin. "No! here we are and here we must get down;" and I heard him add something, which sounded like "they've brought us here, and we will make them descend it!" It was, of course, pitch-dark, and precipices seemed to open at every side.

"Keep the rope tight!" cried my guide, as he proceeded to cut down a narrow knife-edge of ice. I heard a crack, and the mighty sérac seemed to move under my feet.

"Did you feel it move?" I asked Michel.

"Yes, madame."

"Really, I don't much like this," I exclaimed.

"It's all right; come on, madame!" called Cupelin from below.

The arête was finished, but he had to double back and cut along its side in order to reach a couloir which seemed to go in the right direction. After three or four steps down it, it was seen to break off short. We crossed, and found a slippery gully—soft snow over ice which slid from under our feet, but a gentle slope below was reached, and we were soon again on level ground. We trotted on briskly until once more brought to a halt.

"Another sérac?"

"Yes, madame; and this time it seems too steep to get down, we must return a little, and try to turn it to the left."

We did so, and had not gone five minutes before exactly the same thing happened again. Four times were we brought to a full stop by these icy walls; and our zigzags must have looked very comical by day-light. At last came a place where we could jump, and from henceforth we were fairly on the plateau of the Glacier de Gorne. How cold it was! The wind blew the snow into our faces, a very different kind of snow to that which we had found while mounting to the St. Théodule. There it had been hard as snow could be, but here we sunk deeply into the floury substance, and the fatigue was more than doubled. Whenever the slopes faced the south, there the snow was in good condition, but to the north it was as soft as possible. The northern face of the Matterhorn, turned

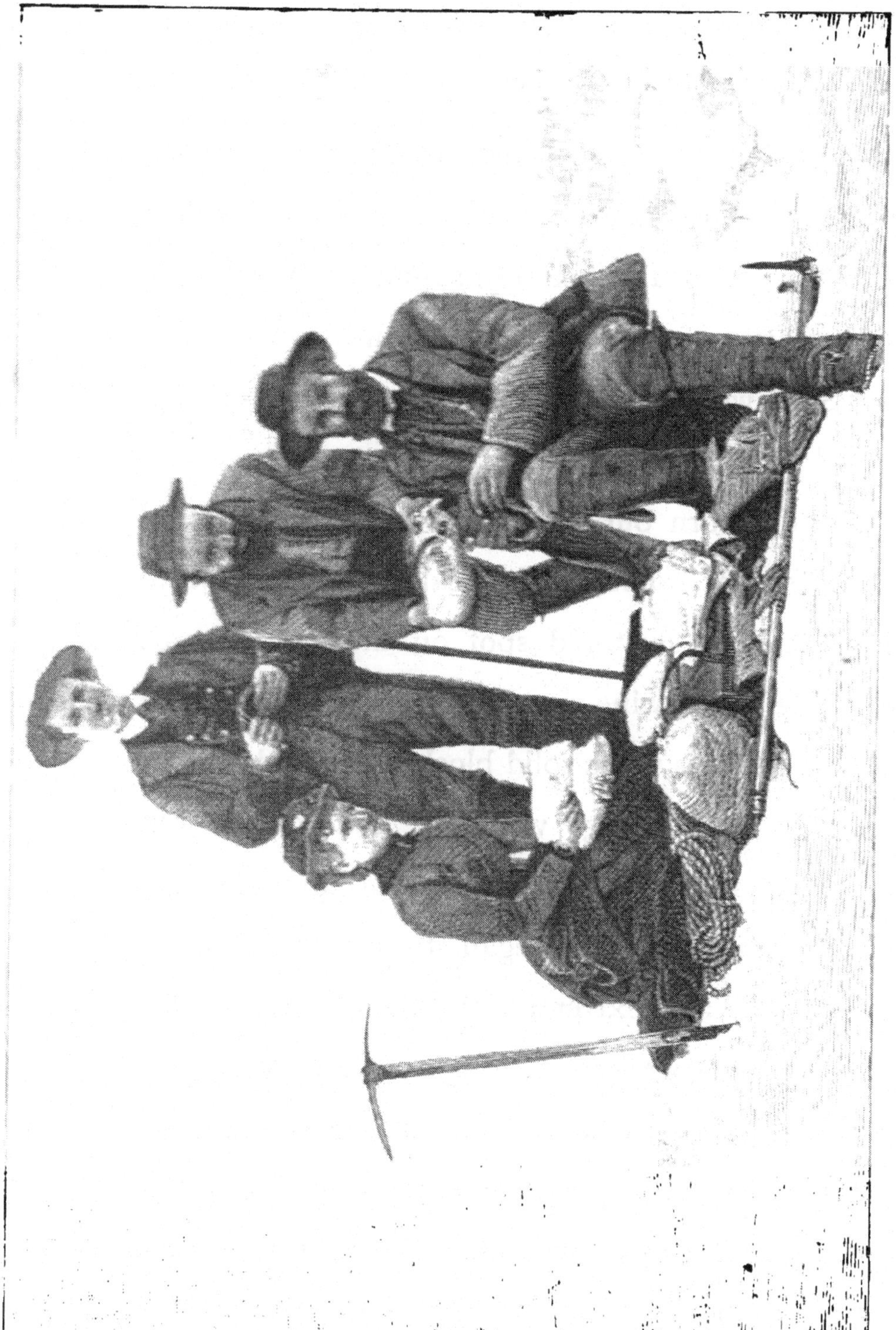

towards Zermatt, was white from top to bottom, while there was hardly more snow on the Italian side than is usually found in summer. Very long and wearisome did the plateau seem.

"Shall we never turn our backs on the Riffelhorn!" exclaimed Auguste.

We did turn our backs, however, in process of time, to that quaint little peak, and sat down to breakfast in a sheltered spot on the snow-covered moraine. Our wine was not yet frozen, but Signor Sella's Marsala was a solid block of ice, and biscuits were the only things which we could eat. The plateau had been monotonous, as I have said, and the slopes which we began to mount after our repast were also extremely tiresome. Still, we felt that, on them, we were making a little progress, and any change was welcomed. So far the cold, though intense, had been bearable, and the wind could be resisted. But as we ascended the cold grew more and more penetrating, and the wind seemed turning to a positive gale. Still we walked upward and upward, while summit after summit sank below and even the Matterhorn seemed almost on a level with us. Mont Blanc was well seen, and the beautiful Graian Alps. Not a cloud anywhere, but a woolly-looking mist which crept up the Glacier de Lion, and hung like a veil against the Italian side of the Cervin. So far my men had not uttered a word as to the cold. The other guides had already grumbled once or twice to them. They had taken the lead a few minutes before, and, when a more furious gust than we had yet felt, made me exclaim, "If we persist we shall all be frozen," they one and all declined to advance a single step further. My guide, whose advice I asked, replied, "We can always try, but I don't think that it will be possible to pass the arête in such a hurricane, and it would be more prudent to descend."

Signor Sella, ever the most courageous, said that he did not feel cold, and would like to continue;

but his men were utterly incapable of following, and refused point-blank. As we were talking, I saw Michel's eyes opening to their widest extent.

"The nose of madame, the nose of madame!" he screamed, and to my astonishment every one began rubbing my poor nose with all their force.

"What is the matter?" I asked.

"Rub, rub hard!" was all the answer I got.

Presently the amount of rubbing which it received seemed so satisfy them, for Cupelin exclaimed,—

"Ah, it's beautiful now!"

"Beautiful! what do you mean?" I inquired.

"Yes," answered my guide; "it's now getting quite black!"

At length they enlightened me. It seemed that my nose had got frost-bitten; that its turning white was the first sign of the catastrophe, and getting black afterwards showed that it was cured. I felt no pain, owing to the intense cold, when it came to, but it burnt as if held before a fire for several days afterwards. Remaining in such a spot was worse than useless. Signor Sella had a thermometer, and quickly took the temperature. The thermometer sank instantaneously as low as it could go (13° below zero, Fahrenheit), but all were agreed that there were many more degrees of cold. We were then close to the beginning of the arête. We turned and fled down the slopes as fast as we could run, and only halted when we got some 2000 feet lower, where an enormous sérac, which had fallen from a glacier above, gave us shelter from the wind. We ate something, and Signor Sella photographed the party—a wretched, half-frozen crew, muffled in shawls and foulards. In another hour we found a dry and charming rock, on which we placed ourselves for a ten-minutes' rest. Some more biscuits were disposed of. Chicken, soup, champagne, in fact, everything, except the cognac, was frozen as hard as a stone. Every time anything had been poured into the glass, half of it had frozen instantaneously to its sides. It was now a queer medley of white and red wines in layers, one over the other. Our feet, exposed to the sun on the dry rock, began to smart suspiciously; and next day we heard that Marquinaz had both feet badly frost-bitten when he arrived on the Col that evening, and Bic's ear was also frozen. My men did not suffer. On the Gorne glacier below, Signor Sella photographed us once more, the Matterhorn at our backs. It will be easily understood that, after being nearly frozen on Monte Rosa, we were not inclined to repeat the process, with a "quite" instead of a "nearly" on the Matterhorn. I had always feared that the month of March is the coldest month in the year in the mountains, and I now had had but too ample proof of the fact. Almost any amount of cold is supportable without a wind; but when there *is* a wind, it changes the whole question. Besides, to ascend the Matterhorn from Breuil in one day was hardly practicable. Fifteen hours would have to be allowed for the ascent, and twelve for the descent, and there was not a sufficient amount of daylight at that season. In such unsettled weather, sleeping in the cabin[2] would have been madness. If a storm came on, the descent would be rendered impracticable, perhaps for weeks. The cabin contains no stove, and is not by any means a comfortable one. The lower one, which will be completed next season below the Great Tower, will be furnished with a stove, plenty of sheepskins, &c., and descent will be quite safe, should bad weather come on.

Prudence overruled valour, and we prepared to say good-bye to Signor Sella, and our hopes of the Matterhorn for that season. The Italians intended to return to the Col St. Théodule, and we decided to descend to Zermatt. Auguste was

[2] The cabin on the Italian side of the mountain is placed at a height of 13,664 feet.

attached to the end of Signor Sella's caravan, and had orders to come down next morning with A—— and Carrel. I could not bring myself to ascend that tiresome slope leading to the Col, and spend another night like the last. We struck off to the right and tramped across the plateau for an hour or so, till we came to some slopes, half grass, half snow, up which we had to go. Once on the top the snow became again atrocious, and we plunged, rather than walked, towards the Riffel. Soon we passed it and sought the couloir below. We were in a hurry, as Cupelin was anxious to find tracks before dark, as a good path would save us both time and fatigue. Of course, just because we were hurried, the snow suddenly got hard again, and cutting had to be resorted to. Finally we got on to a gentler slope, glissaded down it, and were in the wished for tracks before nightfall. Once on the path, we could run, and Zermatt was reached at eight o'clock. We went straight to the hotel,

Monte Rosa, hoping to find some of the domestics there, as had been the case when my guide with Mr. C. passed through the winter before. No such good fortune for us, however. All the hotels, even the Post, were shut. Zermatt seemed already asleep. After a good hunt, we found a man.

Cupelin hailed him in French. He answered in German.

"Ask him where we can find rooms," said my guide.

I did so, but only got, "Ich weiss nicht! alles ist geschlossen!" in answer.

While we were talking another man came up, and Cupelin recognized him as the proprietor of a café. This worthy mortal, Ignace Biner by name, volunteered to do his best for us, and took us to his house, where he and his excellent wife treated us with great hospitality. A room was quickly got ready for me and the scrupulous cleanliness of the whole place was delightful. He sent for bread, then for eggs, somewhere else for a kid, and made me really very comfortable. How pleasant a good twelve-hours' sleep was after the perpetual hurry of the last seven days! Early next morning our landlord went with a telescope to a neighbouring height, to see if A—— with Carrel and Auguste could be seen. Zermatt had tried to frighten me about them, and had talked mysteriously of avalanches, the cold on the Col, the dangers of mountains in the winter, &c., in a way which excited my scorn, for, as they had never tried the mountains at that season, and we had almost lived in them for the last two months, my opinion was perhaps likely to be the most correct of the two. Nevertheless, in spite of all the imaginary perils, A—— and her two guides were seen high above, on the hillside, walking rapidly. Very soon they joined us, with tremendous appetites and faces burnt crimson from the wind. It appeared that there had been a fearful gale during the night which made the cabin literally rock. Their wood had run short, but Carrel ferreted out some planks, which they burnt. The Italian guides had arrived dreadfully tired, and suffered much from their frost-bites. They were preparing to leave for Valtournanche when A—— started.

Sunday was spent quietly at Zermatt, and our good host brought out his fine collection of stones and dried flowers to amuse us. One specimen of crystal, like an emerald, but of a lighter colour, especially struck us. Biner said that he had sent a piece to Paris, but that no one could tell exactly what it was, none like it had ever been found before. He gave us each a pretty little lump in souvenir of our visit.

Monday morning, at six o'clock, we took leave of Zermatt and the beautiful Matterhorn, on which the sun was rising and tinting with pink. We had ordered two sledges, and proceeded to pack ourselves into them. The road was in a condition simply indescribable. Enormous avalanches filled the valley, and a way had been cut through them leaving a wall of ice on each side. In the middle was a rut, and into it one runner of the sledge invariably went, the vehicle, of course, quite on one side all the time. We dared not cling to the edge of the vehicle, for fear of cutting our hands against the walls of ice. It was a puzzle, and required the balancing power of a Blondin, to prevent ourselves slipping out. We had started a little in advance of the sledge containing the guides, and were on a particularly bad bit of road. Our conveyance was in the act of falling over on its side, and I put out my foot to stop myself from getting under it. The whole weight of the sledge, A——, and the driver came on my unlucky foot, and I thought for a moment that it was crushed into a jelly. Cupelin came up breathless, scolded the driver for starting off at such a pace, and clung on behind, jumping down and holding the sledge in its place when the road was very bad, till we got to St. Nicholas. As for the others, they were also upset once or twice, but, being unencumbered by rugs, they hopped out whenever they saw the vehicle lurching over.

It was a cloudless day, but bitterly cold, and we were not sorry to leave the sledge at St. Nicholas, and be on our feet once more. We walked down to Visp, and a lovely walk it was. The torrents were fringed with great blocks of clearest ice, which took most fantastic forms, sometimes in round balls, sometimes like a gigantic fish, and sometimes in long icicles. The fine peak of the Weisshorn reminded me a little of the Aiguille Vert from the Col de Chardonnet. Farther down the valley the snow was left behind, and flowers, white and blue, peeped out from the hedges. I gathered a large bouquet of them, and, in consequence, got to Visp just as the 12.30 train was leaving for Vernayaz. Never mind! We had thoroughly enjoyed our walk, and now for breakfast.

I opened the visitors' book which lay on the table in the dining-room of the Hôtel de Soleil. The first words which caught my eye were, "Try the trout." We ordered some, and only regretted that a dozen were not forthcoming instead of only two. However, the good beefsteak which followed somewhat compensated us.

We spent that night at Vernayaz, and next day crossed the Salvan to Chamonix. This pretty and interesting route is not nearly so well known as it deserves. Many persons who put their necks in imminent peril while driving over that most unsafe road called the Tête Noir, would, I am sure, be both surprised and delighted, did they ride over to Chamonix by Finhaut and Salvan. It is far more picturesque than the other road, and the view which it commands is much more extensive. It is practicable for small carriages with two wheels, but I do not recommend this mode of traversing it. The path, we found, was in good condition, in rather too good condition, in fact, for the hard and frozen earth was very tiring to walk on, and produced a stiffness of the limbs which did not disappear for some days afterwards. Snow began to fall as we left Chatelard, and continued till at half-past four o'clock we entered Chamonix.

"Our last excursion for the season," remarked the guides, "and, as usual, we've brought the good people here bad weather."

CHAPTER XI.

CONCLUSION.

CHAPTER XI.

CONCLUSION.

The difference between winter and summer in the Alps—Best provisions to take—Our method of preventing our wine from freezing—Many drawbacks which will be removed should mountaineering in winter become popular—A tribute to the ability of my guides.

IN concluding I must add a few particulars as to mountaineering in winter, which can be more readily given here than had I inserted them in the account of our excursions. I have several times remarked upon the fact that on no occasion during the months of January and February did we actually suffer from cold. It must not be supposed, however, that the temperature in the heights is the same in winter as in summer. In summer the nights are cold; the days, when without wind and clouds, excessively hot. The variations of temperature are far more marked in summer than in winter, and the difference between early morning and the rest of the day very great. In winter I have often taken off my jacket soon after starting, and not put it on again during the remainder of the course. At that season the sun shines for such a limited number of hours, and one is so seldom fully exposed to it, that one does not suffer from the heat. For that reason, the cold is much less felt than with the same lowness of temperature it would be in summer. The face gets but very slightly burnt, and the eyes much less heated than in summer.

Now as to my manner of carrying the wine and provisions. The former I place in two large tin gourds. These are enclosed in flannel bags, stuffed with cotton wool, and are packed in a knapsack. Even with these precautions, the wine has been frozen once or twice, at the end of the day. The provisions seldom freeze to any extent. Biscuits and cognac seem quite proof against congelation as far as my experience goes.

No doubt, if winter ascents become popular, the châlets will be better arranged for that season, more especially as to the heating of the bed-rooms. This could easily be managed, and would do away with the greatest source of discomfort which will be found. Another, hardly less, is the state of the roads. Not the high roads, which are always kept in good order, but the char roads, upon which one must often walk for hours, through deep snow, and without the vestige of a track.

I have not concealed the fact that mountaineering in winter is, undoubtedly, much more tiring than in summer. During the latter season, a ride of two or three hours will considerably lessen the fatigue, and take one up several thousand feet. In winter, this is out of the question. Of course, in summer, the heat is often very trying, but the snow is more frequently in good condition, and walking on it demands less exertion.

Many more precautions against avalanches of snow have to be taken in winter, but the danger of falling stones is almost nil. The descents, as for instance, those from Pierrepointue, Montanvert, Lognon, &c., are often delightful, and can be accomplished in far less time than is required in summer, and absolutely without fatigue.

And then, with what fervour is the winter tourist greeted! The inn-keepers strain every nerve to make him comfortable. They hope that he is the harbinger of a new era, and that, perhaps, some day, the francs will flow in January or February, as they do in July and August. I cannot end without expressing my admiration of the consummate skill, strength, good temper, and cheerfulness displayed by my guides on every occasion. Never have I seen them for an instant at fault, whether in finding their way down some crevassed glacier in pitch darkness, or in avoiding the various obstacles which the great mass of winter snow often placed in our way.

And now my ramblings during the winter of 1882-83 are over, and I look forward to the coming summer. Yet, pleasant though it may be, I do not expect anything more enjoyable than my winter excursions in the High Alps.

APPENDIX.

APPENDIX A.

COLD *VERSUS* HEAT AS A CURE OF CONSUMPTION.

I DON'T think that a few words will be out of place here, referring to the difference which I, as an invalid sent by my doctor to Algiers, Hyères, Mentone, and Meran, and going on my own account, and according to my own reasoning powers, to heights and bracing air, found between these two *regimes*. At Algiers I felt languid, disinclined to take much exercise. Driving chilled me. The difference between the sun and the shade was very trying. I caught cold easily. I did not sleep well, and my appetite was not good. The objections to Hyères were the same, though in a less degree. The wind which prevailed there was, however, most objectionable, and the following winter I tried the more sheltered Mentone. There, the climate certainly was better, but still I was not satisfied, and found that, on leaving in the spring,

I had lost several pounds' weight. From there I went to Meran, a beautiful little town in the Tyrol, crowded with Germans and hotels, which rival each other in the vile quality of their respective *cuisines*, and the toughness of the meat which their proprietors expect one to eat. I remained two months, and was convinced, at the end of that time, that the place did not suit me. Switzerland, I knew, agreed with me, for I had spent several weeks at Chamonix[1] the summer before, and had never been so strong in my life as during that time. Doctors of highest repute had advised me in June to leave London and try Interlaken and Montreux. I had carried out their orders, and gone to both of these places. I grew weaker and weaker (if possible), and at last, in desperation, determined to take the management of my health into my own hands. Most fortunately—I may say providentially—some people arrived from Chamonix at the hotel where I was staying. I was then hesitating as to whither I would wend my steps. "Go to Chamonix," was the advice they gave me. I took it, and, by easy stages—to Vernayaz—to Tête Noir—to Argentière—I was transported there. The fresh mountain air seemed to put new life into me. In a few days I could

[1] Chamonix is in the Department of Haute-Savoie; but I think it may be classed under the heading of "Switzerland."

leave my sofa, and sit out in the pine woods. Short drives, and then rides, followed, till, at last, I undertook my first glacier excursion, mentioned in the preface. When I left Chamonix, in August, it was with health restored, and one stone ten pounds of weight gained. But, once more in the valleys, I began to lose my energy and strength, and, after another winter at Mentone, I began seriously to turn my thoughts towards the discovery of a winter place in the mountains. The summer was once more spent in the Alps, and the same results followed as in the preceding year. At the conclusion of the season I announced my intention of spending the winter in Switzerland. Doctor—friends—every one exclaimed that it was madness. I, who had been on the borders of consumption, to think of anything so imprudent. At least if I thought that the Riviera did not suit me, let me not expose myself to the intense cold of Davos or St. Moritz. I compromised the matter, and went to Montreux. The rest is known to my readers. I have given this little sketch of the various influences of climate upon my own health, as I feel sure that it will interest many who have not yet found the air to suit them. I do not, however, consider that high mountain air in winter is suitable to the patient who, in an advanced state of lung disease, lacks sufficient strength to enable him to take the amount of exercise required to obtain sufficient fresh air. Sleighing is very catch-cold work, and I think that high places do good only to persons who can walk for an hour or so, and can thereby gain the power of sleep, and the appetite which mountain air produces in those with whom it agrees. In all the bitter cold to which I have been often exposed, never once have I caught the slightest chill, and yet, at Mentone, three colds were my average for the winter, and blisters, and other long-since discarded remedies were brought into constant requisition. The entire absence of damp, and the purity of the air, no doubt account for this fact.

A short time ago, I had the following conversation with a mountaineer of many years' experience, "How is it," he asked me, "that you can walk for hours in the mountains without fatigue, and make all these ascents, when your constitution is by no means a strong one, and, as every doctor whom you have consulted has told you, your predisposition to the fatal disease of consumption—which is so much developed in your family—is so great?" "It must be the air," I answered; "have you never heard of similar cases?" "I have," he replied, "and both my two friends, with whom just the same results from the same treatment followed, gave me, when I questioned them, the same answer which you have done."

"Were they, then, also consumptive?" I inquired. "Yes," he said, "and not only consumptive, but, in one case, the disease was in such an advanced condition, that my young friend's doctor had told him that a year more was all he could expect to live. On hearing this, Mr. —— went to Switzerland. He got a little stronger there. Some friends invited him to make a few expeditions with them. He did so, got better, and soon began mountaineering on his own account. At the end of a year, hardly a trace of his malady remained, and at the end of the second year he was completely cured." "And the other?" I asked. "Very much the same history," he replied, "but he had not been quite so ill at the beginning." One more case, this time *apropos* of general debility and weakness more than of consumption. Last summer an American arrived at Chamonix in very feeble health, had been so for years, he said. He remained for some time at the Hôtel d'Angleterre, and then, by my advice, tried Montanvert. He managed to walk up there, stayed a week, and finally departed over the Col du Géant to Courmayeur, a trudge of from ten to twelve hours. I could cite many other cases in which similar results have followed, but I think I have said enough to convince those who have not themselves tried it, of the miraculous effects of mountain air.

APPENDIX B.

MOUNTAIN WALKERS AND VALLEY WALKERS.

I HAVE often dwelt on the fatigue I experienced during our long and unavoidable walks in the valleys, either before or after ascents. Now, to the inexperienced it may seem odd, that three hours walking on a flat road should tire one more than six uphill. Yet such is the case. I have many times discussed this question with men accustomed to the mountains, and the conclusion which I have drawn from their opinions and my own observations is that, on flat and smooth ground the pace is much faster, the foot is always placed in exactly the same position, and, therefore, the same muscles are constantly brought into use, the air is less sustaining in the valleys, and earth far less elastic than ice or good snow. There is the same difference between walking on roads or ascending on snow slopes, and between mounting over the latter or on rocks. On rocks the arms come into play, and the feet are never placed twice in precisely the same manner. The progress is very slow, and the occupation contains plenty of variety which amuses and distracts the mind. My guides say that the English are "terrible" in the valleys. "We have our knapsacks and they give us their coats; then they stride on in front, perhaps under a broiling sun, and they can't understand why they can walk faster than we do; *c'est les vallées qui tuent.*"

APPENDIX C.

CHAMONIX IN WINTER.

SHOULD any one want to visit this place in winter, the following particulars may be useful. A diligence runs daily from Geneva to Salanches. The night may be spent there not uncomfortably, and the journey continued next day. No diligence runs between Chamonix and Salanches after October 1 and before May 1. A carriage to hold four inside and one on the box can be hired at Geneva for the entire journey—cost 110 francs; the horses will be changed twice, and a sledge provided from Chatelard should there be too much snow to proceed all the way to Chamonix on wheels. The post passes daily, doing the journey partly by night. Several hotels remain open at Chamonix all the winter, including the Hôtel Mont-Blanc, des Alpes, Couttet, and de l'Union.[1]

---

[1] I cannot speak too highly of the comfort of the Hôtel Mont-Blanc, at which I stayed during part of the winter.

Every comfort can be had from Geneva at Chamonix in winter. Fish, all kinds of meat and game, &c.; and the rooms are heated with stoves, and protected with double windows from the cold.

I see no reason why Chamonix should not, some day, rival Davos and St. Moritz as a winter resort. Two charming châlets, on the hill-side above the town, facing due south, are being turned into a casino. A good band will be hired for the summer season, which will play every evening, on the prettily laid-out terraces in front. There will also be a reading-room, and should the thing succeed (as it ought to), an opera-house will be added. In winter this would be even a greater resource than in summer, and land flooded for skating, and everything else which could contribute to the amusement of the visitors, would certainly be arranged by the energetic natives of this civilized little place, did it come into fashion at that season. That it will do so, sooner or later, I feel persuaded.

A railway is to be opened in a few weeks at La Roche near Bonneville (Ligne Annecy-Genève), which will shorten the drive from Geneva to Chamonix by three hours.

APPENDIX D.

THE AIGUILLE DU TACUL.

I SHOULD like to say something about an easy ascent in the chain of Mont Blanc, which was done for the first time some three or four years ago, and which really merits attention. I refer to the Pic or Aiguille du Tacul. This mountain is well seen from Montanvert. It stands on the junction of the Mer de Glace and the Glacier de Léchaud, and, when ascended by the Glacier des Periades, presents no difficulties to the tolerably experienced. A couloir, guarded by a small bergschrund, and then an arête of sound rocks, with good foothold and handhold, lead from the glacier mentioned above to the summit. The view is a magnificent one, for the spectator stands in a perfect circle of snowy peaks, from which glittering glaciers roll their icy waves. The rocky walls of the Grandes Jorasses are unique from this point, and the chain of Mont Rose and other distant summits appear above on every side. The height is about 11,500 feet. In ascending, should your guides not have been up before, all they must do, once off the Glacier du Géant (which they may quit soon after it joins the Mer de Glace), is to bear very much to the right, till they come in sight of the couloir. The couloir cannot be mistaken, and the way from henceforth is quite plain. On the other side of the couloir is the steep slope up which we came when making the first passage of the Col. During the summer I had ascended the Aiguille, and was much surprised to notice the tracks of Mr. C———'s caravan, who had done this mountain in the winter. The line of tracks was well marked, and there is no doubt that they were really those of his party. I had certain knowledge that no one had been up since.

APPENDIX E.

THE ROPE.

During my winter excursions the rope was called into constant requisition. Some of my readers may consider that we used it too frequently, and on places where so much caution was not required. It may be so, and yet I still maintain that this precaution is never a foolish one. On mule paths, in the winter season changed into smooth and often very steep slopes of snow, the rope prevented many an awkward slip, and saved us much time. On glaciers which in summer are ice, but were then covered with snow, which hid their crevasses, the rope was invariably used. Even to cross the Mer de Glace we were tied up, and very thankful I felt that the precaution had been taken, when one of the party suddenly sank to his waist in a concealed pitfall. I invariably use the English Alpine Club rope, with red thread inside. It is light, and can thoroughly be depended upon. Some guides are very careless about ropes, and I have seen one who is well known and considered first-class, tie up a party with a rope which he had used the day before for attaching his horse to a cart. My guide was entreated by some of his comrades to sell an old rope which he no longer used, and he finally destroyed it to prevent any danger arising should it get into any one else's possession. Have your own rope, and never be persuaded to use another, unless it is of a quality known to you, and has been carefully examined by yourself

APPENDIX F.

CONDITION OF THE SNOW IN WINTER.

We very seldom found the snow in good condition during the winter season in the heights. The heat of the sun, which will sometimes, in summer, consolidate by partial melting freshly fallen snow in the space of forty-eight hours, was wanting. On slopes facing the south the snow, after several days' fine weather, was good, but everywhere to the north it was of an execrable quality. For several days fine weather was a rarity during the winter of 1882-83. Five days was the longest duration of unbroken weather, with the exception of a fortnight from February 19 to March 5. During that time there was only one cloudy day, but the terrific gale which raged under those blue skies, in the upper regions, was even more of an obstacle to mountaineering than had mists prevailed. In the corresponding season of 1881-82 the weather was very different. For three months it was quite settled, and there was but little snow on the ground. Nevertheless, my guide has told me that during the excursions he made in January and February with Mr. C——, they never once found what would, in summer, be considered good snow. The wind, of course, helps to harden it, but really good snow to both north and south cannot be expected when the small amount of heat which it receives from the sun in the winter months is remembered. When ascending through forests, we generally found the snow very soft. In almost every walk which takes one off the road and up the slopes an ice-axe, however, in some places is an absolute necessity. While going to Montanvert, and just before turning the corner beyond which the first glimpse of the hotel is obtained, quite half an hour's cutting is almost always required. Ten minutes from Breuil I cut for a quarter of an hour straight up the arête above the hotel. There were no traces of crevasses as far as the Col, therefore the rope was not used; the snow was as hard as snow can be. On the opposite, or northern side, several snow-bridges broke under our weight, but, as I mentioned before, we were roped on leaving the hut, and the cord kept well stretched all the time.

APPENDIX G.

HOTELS AND INNS IN THE ALPINE VALLEYS.

WITH the exception of Valtournanche and Zermatt, we could invariably get what we wanted at the different inns where we either had breakfast, spent the night, or from which we took our provisions. The Hôtel des Alpes, at Orsières was especially well provided, and the numerous dishes which came up for my dinner on the two occasions when I spent the night there, really astonished me. Bourg St. Pierre, also, was much better supplied than I expected, and Chatillon was thoroughly comfortable. At Chatelard (Hôtel Suisse) I also spent a night, and was given an excellent dinner. Our breakfast at the Hôtel Soliel, Visp, is still fresh in my memory. Vernayaz, of course, was highly civilized. As for Valtournanche, I have already spoken of its two veal cutlets. And at Zermatt we should have fared badly, had we not had the good fortune to meet with the capable and energetic Ignace Biner. Moral—take plenty of potted meats.

APPENDIX H.

A HIGH LEVEL ROUTE ALONG THE CHAIN OF MONT BLANC.

WHY has no one yet done a high level route along the chain of Mont Blanc? It is quite practicable, and would be an interesting excursion. Here is a plan for two routes, compiled by my guide and myself. The idea was his.

Route I. (Difficult.)

1st day. From Pavillon de Trelatete over Col Infranchisable to cabin on les Aiguilles Grise.

2nd day. From cabin over Mont Blanc to Grands Mulets.

3rd day. From Grands Mulets over Col du Midi to Col du Géant.

4th day. Ascend Aiguille du Géant and descend to Montanvert (or ascend Aiguille du Tacul and cross Col du Tacul to Pierre à Beranger or Couvercle).

5th day. Cross Col des Courtes to Lognon.

6th day. From Lognon over Col d'Argentière to Orsières.

Route II. (Easier.)

1st day. Over Col de Miage to cabin on les Aiguilles Grise.

2nd day. From cabin over Mont Blanc to Grands Mulets.

3rd day. From Grand Mulets over Col du Midi to Montanvert (or along Plan des Aiguilles).

4th day. From Montanvert over Col des Grands Montets (ascend Aiguille) to Lognon.

5th day. From Lognon over Col du Chardonnet and Fenêtre de Saleinaz by Glacier d'Orny to Orsières (or by Glacier du Tour to Chamonix).

For day 1 (routes I. and II.) it would be advisable to order a porter from Courmayeur to ascend to the cabin with provisions, blankets, and wood.

For day 2 (route I.) another porter should be sent to the Col du Géant.

If the travellers spend the night at Pierre à Beranger on the Couvercle, a porter could be ordered from Montanvert (there is a telegraph office at the hotel). The cabin at the Pierre à Beranger is in such a bad condition that it is preferable to sleep under the rocks outside. I would suggest a tent being kept at Montanvert which travellers could hire and pitch at the Jardin.

APPENDIX I.

A FEW WORDS OF CAUTION.

ONE word as to guides who have been accustomed to the mountains in the winter as compared with those who only know them in summer. There are, it is true, many risks which any guide with common sense would know how to avoid, and which are the natural results of the winter season. But how few guides have that extent of reasoning power, and that almost instinctive knowledge of the different qualities of ice and snow at that time of year which experience in summer ascents alone cannot give them! Therefore (and I cannot urge the point too strongly), if you desire to make winter ascents, take with you, at least, one guide who has tried that sort of work before. Or you may, perhaps, have a really first-rate man who, though without actual experience, has studied the question seriously and intelligently. In that case he ought to be capable of avoiding the risks of winter excursions. One instance, however, will be remembered, of a guide of well-known ability losing his life through want of experience. I allude to the death of Bennen, on the Haut-de-Cry,[1] Canton de Valais. He started with two Englishmen and three natives of Ardon on the 28th of February, 1864, to ascend that mountain. The slope was steep, "a sort of couloir on a large scale," and the snow in a most unstable condition. When 150 feet from the top the crust slipped and the whole party were carried down in the avalanche. One of the Englishmen and Bennen were suffocated. The writer ends his thrilling description with these words:—"Bennen has been accused of rashness in this unfortunate accident. It is not the case. He was misled by the total difference of the state of snow in a winter ascent from what is to be met with in summer."[2]

[1] The summit of the Haut-de-Cry is 9699 feet above the level of the sea.
[2] *The Alpine Journal*, No. 6.

THE END.

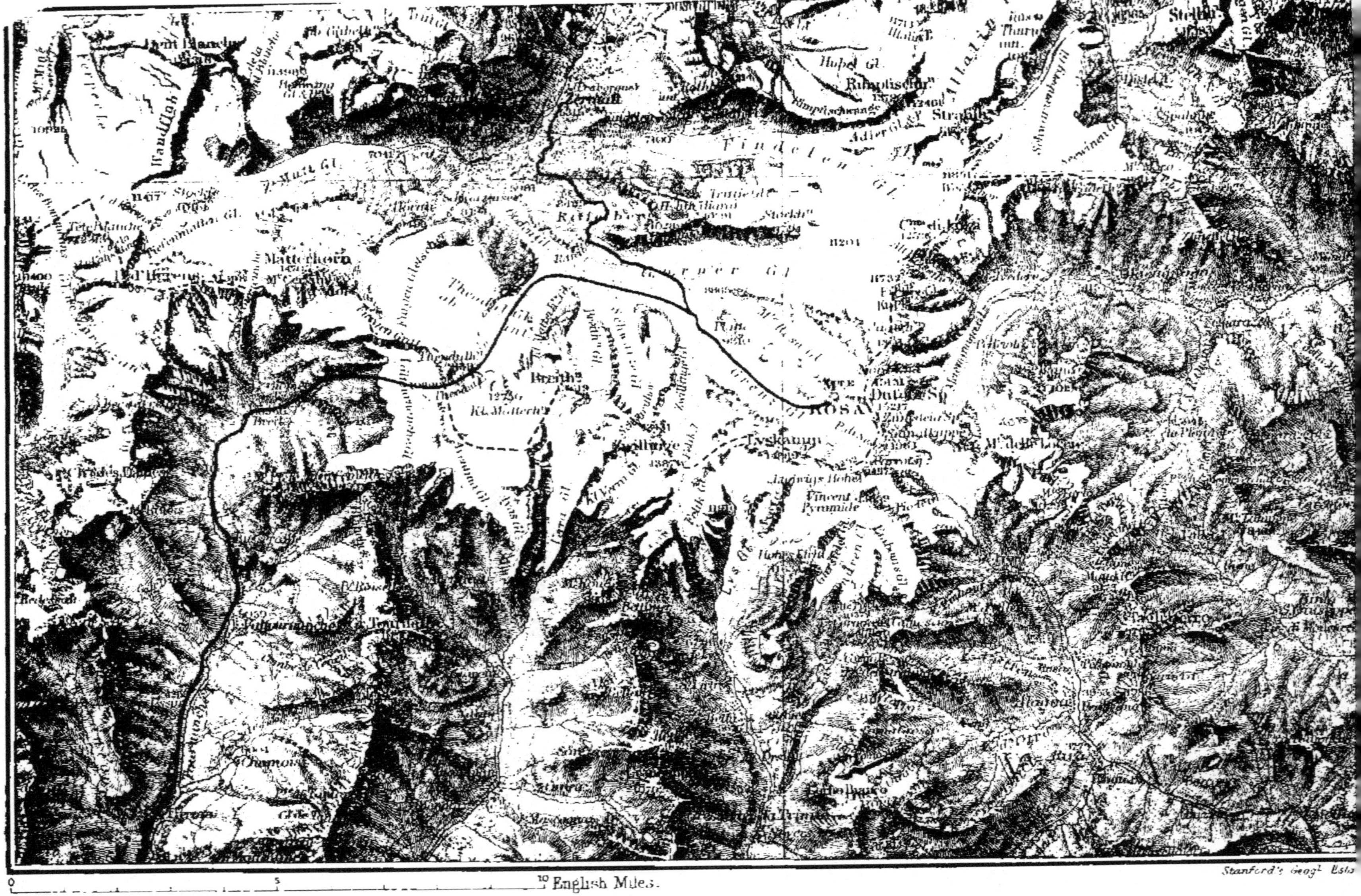

London: Sampson Low & Co.